THE WOODROW WILSON STORY

CATHERINE OWENS PEARE

THE WOODROW WILSON STORY

An Idealist in Politics

THOMAS Y. CROWELL COMPANY • NEW YORK

BY THE AUTHOR

The Helen Keller Story
The FDR Story
The Woodrow Wilson Story

Designed by Albert Burkhardt
Manufactured in the United States of America
by Vail-Ballou Press, Inc., Binghamton, New York
Library of Congress Catalog Card No. 63-9211
Second Printing

ACKNOWLEDGMENTS

I am indebted to Arthur S. Link, Professor of History at Princeton University and editor of The Papers of Woodrow Wilson; to Jonathan Daniels, editor of *The News and Observer* in Raleigh, North Carolina; and to Grace W. Bacon, Reference Librarian at Wesleyan University; all of whom read and criticized portions of my manuscript. I am also indebted to Mrs. Herman K. Peters, Custodian of the Woodrow Wilson Birthplace Foundation, Inc., in Staunton, Virginia, for reading the manuscript.

For special research assistance I wish to thank Mrs. Herbert McK. Smith, President of the Birthplace Foundation; John Cook Wyllie, Librarian at the Alderman Library, University of Virginia; the late President Wilson's niece, Mrs. I. Stuart McElroy, of Richmond, Virginia; Elizabeth S. Hoyt, Research Librarian for the Historical Foundation of the Presbyterian and Reformed Churches and Professor of History at Montreat-Anderson College, Montreat, North Carolina; and the librarians at Davidson College, Davidson, North Carolina; the Public Library of Charlotte and Mecklenburg County, Charlotte, North Carolina; the Richland County Public Library and the South Caroliniana Library, Columbia, South Carolina; the Augusta–Richmond County Public Library, Augusta, Georgia; The Lotos Club, New York City; and the Brooklyn Public Library, Brooklyn, New York.

I am grateful to the following for permission to quote material from the works indicated below:

The Bobbs-Merrill Company, Inc.: *My Memoir,* copyright 1938, 1939 by Edith Bolling Wilson, reprinted by special permission of the publishers.

Doubleday & Company, Inc.: *Woodrow Wilson as I Know Him,* by Joseph P. Tumulty, copyright 1921 by Doubleday, Page & Company.

Harcourt, Brace & World, Inc.: *Roosevelt: The Lion and the Fox,* by James MacGregor Burns, published 1956.

Harper & Row, Publishers, Inc.: *The Public Papers of Woodrow Wilson,* 6 volumes, edited by Ray Stannard Baker and William E. Dodd, published 1926.

Holt, Rinehart and Winston, Inc.: *Woodrow Wilson, An Intimate Memoir,* by Cary T. Grayson, published 1960; and *Life of Woodrow Wilson,* by Josephus Daniels, published 1924.

Houghton Mifflin Company: *The Intimate Papers of Colonel House,* edited by Charles Seymour, published 1926–1928.

Mrs. Eleanor Wilson McAdoo: *The Woodrow Wilsons,* by Eleanor Wilson McAdoo, published by The Macmillan Company, 1937.

McGraw-Hill Book Company, Inc.: *The Ordeal of Woodrow Wilson,* copyright © 1958 by Herbert Hoover.

David McKay Company, Inc.: *Woodrow Wilson,* by Arthur C. Walworth, published by Longmans, Green & Co., 1958, courtesy of David McKay Company, Inc.

The Macmillan Company: *The Autobiography of William Allen*

White, copyright 1946 by The Macmillan Company; and *Woodrow Wilson and the Lost Peace,* by Thomas A. Bailey, copyright 1944 by The Macmillan Company.

Mrs. Rachel Baker Napier and Doubleday & Company, Inc.: *Woodrow Wilson, Life and Letters,* by Ray Stannard Baker, vols. 1 and 2 copyright 1927 by Doubleday & Company, Inc., vols. 3–7 copyright 1931, 1935, 1937, 1939 by Ray Stannard Baker, reprinted by permission of Mrs. Napier and Doubleday & Company, Inc.; and *Woodrow Wilson and World Settlement,* by Ray Stannard Baker, published by Doubleday, Page & Company, 1922.

The Ohio Historical Society: "Woodrow Wilson's First Romance," by George C. Osborn, published in *The Ohio Historical Quarterly,* January 1958.

Princeton University Press: *Wilson, The Road to the White House* (1947); *Wilson, The New Freedom* (1956); and *Wilson, The Struggle for Neutrality* (1960), by Arthur S. Link.

University of North Carolina Press: *My Aunt Louisa and Woodrow Wilson,* by Margaret Axson Elliott, published 1944; and *The Wilson Era,* by Josephus Daniels, published 1944 and 1946.

Contents

THE WOODROW WILSON STORY

1. There Will Be War

A SOLEMN-FACED boy stood on the sidewalk in front of his home, listening to the conversation of adults walking by. Their voices were filled with tension and excitement.

"Lincoln has been elected!"

"Then there will be war!"

Who was Lincoln? What was elected? What was war? The small child turned and bolted up the steps, across the porch, and into the house. He would find out the meaning of this from his father.

But even with a careful explanation the words were beyond the understanding of nearly four-year-old Tommy Wilson. The political tensions that had been gathering for thirty years between the manufacturing North and planting South, between Abolitionist and slaveowner, between Unionist and Secessionist, had not reached him at all until now. He was much too young for *Uncle Tom's Cabin,* and no one had tried to explain John Brown's raid to so young a child.

Today, though, as he raced through the wide halls and big rooms of the red brick manse, Thomas Woodrow Wilson had picked up the contagious excitement that electrified the air. Even his father, stately minister of the First Presbyterian Church of Augusta, Georgia, showed the effect of it.

The excitement did not die down in the weeks that followed. On the day before Christmas, 1860, South Carolina announced her withdrawal from the Union. Ten other states quickly followed, Georgia among them, and the Wilsons found themselves citizens of the Confederate States of America.

Even though they considered themselves Southerners, neither of Tommy Wilson's parents had been born in the South. His father, the Reverend Dr. Joseph Ruggles Wilson, was from Steubenville, Ohio, where his Scottish parents had migrated from the northern part of Ireland. Tommy's mother, Janet Woodrow—called Jessie and sometimes Jeanie—was Scottish too. She had been born in Carlisle, England, where her father was a Presbyterian minister, and had come to America with her family when she was nine.

Joseph Wilson was a learned man, gifted both as a preacher and teacher, and in the first few years of his marriage rose rapidly from one post to another. He began as pastor of a church in Chartier, Pennsylvania; from there he went to teach at Jefferson College and then at Hampden-Sydney College in Virginia. In the summer of 1855 he was made pastor of the First

Presbyterian Church of Staunton, Virginia, and to that city he moved with his young wife and two small daughters, Marion aged five and Anne aged four.

Staunton is a lovely and historic old town, built on a group of steep hills in the Shenandoah Valley of the Blue Ridge Mountain region. The Presbyterian manse is still there, midway up one of the hills, its two-story front facing eastward at 24 North Coalter Street, the hill dropping away from it in the rear to reveal three stories. It is a big square house of brick painted white, the most luxurious home the Wilsons had occupied so far. There is a wide center hall and two big rooms on either side on the street floor, kitchen and storeroom below, four more big rooms on the upper floor, one of them the minister's study. On a fair day Dr. Wilson was very apt to take his work out onto the second-floor porch on the back of the house with its sweeping view of the well house, carriage house, gardens, grazing animals, and beyond them a valley filled with apple orchards that became a riot of blossoms in the spring, and farther away more hills, hills, hills. The beauty of the countryside found its way into his sermons, which he preached with ever increasing power in the church that is now the chapel of Mary Baldwin College.

The Wilsons had lived in the Staunton manse about a year and a half when their third child was born, late at night on the 28th of December, 1856. He was their first son, named Thomas Woodrow Wilson for his grandfather, the Reverend Dr. Thomas Woodrow.

But before Thomas, or Tommy, reached his first birthday, his father was assigned to a still larger and more affluent pulpit in Augusta, Georgia. Tommy's earliest recollection was of the day in Augusta when he stood before the manse and heard someone say, "There will be war."

War did come, beginning officially with the attack upon Fort Sumter the following April, and lasting for four long, destructive years, until Tommy Wilson was eight—old enough to understand such words as President, elected, re-elected, assassinated, cavalry, ammunition, hospitals, prisoners of war, food shortages.

Augusta was much larger than Staunton; Broad Street, its principal thoroughfare, ran for almost two miles through the length of it, with three blocks in the center of town where business houses concentrated. Augusta was highly industrial. Standing at the head of navigation on the Savannah River and in the heart of the cotton- and corn-growing region, it hummed with cotton mills, flour mills, brickworks, and sent its products downriver to Savannah for distribution. All these manufactures meant wealth, and wealth meant that Augusta and the surrounding country were graced with large, beautiful homes, usually gleaming white, many of them fronted with classical columns.

The manse had its white-columned porch, and diagonally across the street from it rose the tall slim steeple of the church hidden in a grove of huge trees. The First Presbyterian Church stands in the center of a tree-filled square bounded by a white picket fence, between Seventh and Sixth Streets, facing on Telfair, which runs parallel to Broad. Its spacious, plain interior with rows of mahogany pews was a restful and comforting place to worship, until the war began. But with the coming of the Civil War one activity after another crowded in upon it. In the first year of hostilities a split occurred in the Presbyterian Church over the question of abolition, and Tommy Wilson's father invited its first Southern Assembly to meet in his church. Dr. Wilson was elected the Permanent Clerk of the Southern Presbyterian Church.

Standing tall and straight in the raised pulpit, his long firm chin ringed with whiskers, Dr. Joseph Ruggles Wilson presented a splendid picture to his son, as Tommy sat in the third pew from the front on the center aisle with his mother and two sisters. Tommy resembled his father somewhat with his high forehead and firm mouth, but his features were sharper, his jaw line longer, his eyes gray, and he was thin and frail.

As a boy of four, five, six, walking in the glow of his father's stalwart personality, Tommy absorbed the valor and vigor of the older man, and tried through his father to understand what went on around him. Dr. Wilson was a man from whom loving care flowed in abundant supply, most abundantly for his own family, and all during the Civil War he gave Tommy the only education the boy received. They sat on the floor together while Dr. Wilson taught Tommy to recognize letters and numbers. As far back as he could remember, Tommy Wilson's father was his hero, teacher, adviser, friend, companion, and playmate.

Dr. Wilson was always willing to read aloud to his whole family, something from the Bible every day, the novels of Charles Dickens, biography, travel. Gay discussions at mealtime, often with visitors, were all part of learning, and often the dictionary had to be brought to the table to settle a fine point.

To the minister's family, church was as constant in their lives as mealtimes, and Tommy watched the congregation turn to his father with the same wholehearted respect and trust that he felt himself. And the member of the congregation who listened to sermons with the frankest adoration was his mother.

Jessie Wilson was not a dramatic personality like her husband. She was sedate and gentle, moving about in her tight bodice and long full skirts with ladylike steps; and she wore her hair parted in the middle with short curls hanging on either side of her face. Her talent was music, and she played the harpsichord and guitar. She taught the children music, played and sang with them, and in the evenings—particularly Sunday evenings—the whole family sang hymns together. Often their song festivals included neighbors and guests, because the minister's wife was hospitable and generous. Tommy had a singing voice and loved the old Scottish songs he learned from his parents as much as visitors did.

Tommy Wilson was shy as a child and drew as much security from his quiet, constant mother as he did from his deep-voiced father. During his earliest days in Augusta he followed her from room to room, upstairs or down, one hand gripping the folds of her skirt. "Mamma's boy, Mamma's boy!" his sisters might taunt him, but he clung and followed all the same.

He clung as they stood in the yard watching the first Augusta volunteer units ride out of town to join the Confederate army.

Augusta was quickly caught up in a wartime turmoil. At first people were gay and confident, cheering the young men drilling in the square—eleven companies in the first few months—shouting wildly for joy when they heard of the early Confederate victory at Manassas. The row of powder works, built along the canal that flowed through town, hummed around the clock, and on a hill that rose to the west of Augusta a huge munitions factory was under way.

The turmoil endured, but the mood changed when the first trainload of sick and wounded was brought back from the front, and Augusta became a hospital town. The First Presbyterian Church, like churches of other denominations in town, had to be used as a hospital. Near it on Telfair and Sixth stood the old Medical College where Confederate surgeons had their offices.

There could be no more clinging to Mother's skirts, because Mother was as busy as every other woman in town, caring for the stricken. If Tommy followed her he would be treated to the revolting odors of gangrene, the sight of fever-glazed eyes, the sounds of pain and grief.

By the second and third years of the war the space in back of Dr. Wilson's church had been enclosed as a prison stockade for captive Union soldiers, and a boy staring through the palings to discover what Yankee monsters looked like would see more misery. Slowly, unconsciously, a definition of war was developing in his mind.

Food became scarcer, and money lost its value, as the tide of war turned against the South. Tommy Wilson never forgot the flavor of soup made from cowpeas. Cowpeas had always been fed to cattle; he hadn't realized that people could eat them at all. Cut plug tobacco became more stable in value than money, and could be used as currency. Men hoarded it. Even Tommy's father had a hoard of cut plug in the attic.

The Wilsons, unyielding Scots, never surrendered their standards or family patterns all during the war. No matter how much war work had to be done, there was always time each day to read the Bible together, to pray, to sing; and whatever they had to eat didn't change their conversations around the meal table. Every Sunday morning Dr. Wilson was in his pulpit, and his wife and three children were in their pew.

Only once was Dr. Wilson known to have shortened the service to a few words when he told his congregation:

"There is a great battle pending, and the Southern army is in desperate need of ammunition. I shall dismiss you at once so that you can all repair to the factory and help roll cartridges."

The startled worshipers obeyed.

Tommy Wilson was nearly eight when President Jefferson Davis came to Augusta. It was toward the end of 1864, and President Davis was making a personal speaking tour to raise Southern morale. The South had been defeated at Vicksburg and Gettysburg, and Union troops under General Sherman had reached Atlanta, Georgia, less than 150 miles away. Shortly after Davis's visit, Augusta heard that Atlanta had been burned and that Sherman was on his march to the sea, robbing, burning, killing, cutting the South in two with a wide path of destruction. Augusta could expect the same. Refugees from Atlanta, Tennessee, and the Carolinas poured into Augusta, fleeing from Sherman's army.

Racing through town with other youngsters, Tommy Wilson watched as the streets were barricaded with huge bales of cotton and barrels of tar were placed on the bridge. Sherman would find Augusta already on fire when he got there, and none of her munitions or machine shops would do him any good.

Running home, bursting into the house, to his

mother, father, fourteen-year-old Marion, ten-year-old Anne, to find out the truth! Was Augusta going to burn? Was Sherman coming here?

"Thank heaven you are home!"

Tommy became big-eyed and silent as dusk gathered and his mother placed a lighted lamp near a window to burn all night.

Augusta waited, anxious and tense; many sat in continuous prayer. What men were left in the town rode out into the nearby woods and fields to watch for the first signs of attack.

The attack never came. Sherman and his army took an almost straight route out to Savannah. From there he turned northward to destroy Columbia, the capital of South Carolina. The following April came the surrender at Appomattox, and the Confederacy was no more.

A few weeks later Tommy Wilson saw Jefferson Davis being escorted along Broad Street in an open carriage by a body of cavalry—a prisoner of war—his face filled with grief. He had been captured in southern Georgia and brought to Augusta to be taken aboard a barge down the Savannah River to a larger vessel that would carry him to Virginia where he would be imprisoned for two years at Fortress Monroe.

Surrender brought tragic changes to life in Augusta and to life in all the Confederate states. It brought fear of reprisal too. President Lincoln declared that the government would take a merciful attitude toward the defeated South, that he favored conciliation and rebuilding and a healing of the nation's wounds; but orators in Congress who opposed Lincoln were shouting for vengeance and punishment. A few days after Appomattox came news of President Lincoln's assassination. Shouts for vengeance grew louder. But soon there came the further news that Lincoln's successor, President Andrew Johnson, intended to carry out Lincoln's compassionate attitude toward the South.

President Johnson was himself a Southerner; he wanted the war-ruined South restored wisely. He granted pardons to Southern leaders who were willing to take an oath of allegiance to the United States government. Georgia and other Southern states were given provisional civilian governments until order could be restored out of the confusions that always follow a war.

The most tragic social conditions were caused by the sudden freeing of the Negroes, a third of Augusta's population of 15,000. They swarmed through the streets, confused and unable to provide for themselves, huddling in barns for shelter, falling ill or starving, too few of them educated enough to provide leadership to their own people. Tommy saw the Freedmen's Bureau, created as an emergency agency by the federal government, distribute food, begin schools, and teach the former slaves why they must provide for themselves. But along with the agents of the Freedmen's Bureau Tommy also saw the arrival of the cheap politician, the carpetbagger, come to fleece and exploit the dislocated.

Tommy was going on nine when the war ended. He and his favorite companions—Pleasant Stovall, Will Fleming, Joseph Lamar who lived in the house next to the manse—liked to wander about town to see every interesting thing there was to see—down along the Savannah River where mills stood idle, or upriver toward the region called Sand Hills. There Aunt Marion, his mother's sister, and Uncle James Bones lived. Their house was a second home to Tommy. His cousin Jessie Bones was enough of a tomboy to be allowed to play with them at times.

But at nine Tommy Wilson had never attended formal school, and as soon as it was possible he and several other lads were enrolled in a private school in rooms over the post office. The headmaster was Joseph T. Derry, who had just returned to Augusta after serving in the Confederate army.

The discipline of the classroom was an unpleasant surprise. Sitting stiffly at a desk learning Latin verbs and history, practicing penmanship and bookkeeping, was not like sprawling on the parlor floor and reading for pure joy. Latin verbs seemed to have so little bearing on life that Tommy Wilson decided he must be a poor memorizer and let it go at that.

When the school was moved to larger quarters near the river, the young students were overjoyed. This was much better! Here they could play hide-and-seek among the bales of cotton in a nearby warehouse, a far more interesting pastime than the lessons that Headmaster Derry was so in earnest about. Interest in their lessons fell to absolute zero when they heard that a circus was coming to town.

Off they went with the excited crowds along Broad Street to watch the parade, a huge lumbering elephant in the vanguard. It was the first really happy event that had happened in Augusta since before the war, and who could remember that far back? School could wait! It would have to!

It would also have to be faced the next day, and Tommy and his friends found Headmaster Derry more in earnest than ever, with a stout cane in his hand. Oh, they were in for it, they knew. The cane was applied to the seat of every pair of trousers that had played hooky.

School a century ago was not designed to discover the depths in Thomas Woodrow Wilson. In the years before his teens he was an out-of-doors boy. He and Stovall organized the Lightfoot Club, essentially a baseball team, so that they could play other teams in the area. Sometimes they disguised themselves as Indians and played at war games, often chasing and plaguing the Negro children.

Or they forced Tommy's cousin, Jessie Bones, to allow herself to be tied and burned at the stake while they jumped and yelped around her. One day they were hunters and ordered Jessie up into a tree to be a squirrel. Tommy, the dauntless brave, shot an arrow at her, and to his horror she fell out of the tree, unconscious. Gathering her up in his arms, he bore her home to his Aunt Marion and said:

"I am a murderer. It wasn't an accident. I killed her."

He was deeply relieved when cold water revived his victim, for to Tommy truth was truth. If he had killed, he had killed, with no begging excuses. That was how he learned it every hour of every day at home and in church, in small incidents and great. Worship to the Wilsons was no idle form. God was a vital presence in every waking minute of their lives; the Bible was read so that its meaning and guidance could be searched out and absorbed. When Tommy Wilson was confronted with a decision at any time in his life, his childhood religious training was his automatic resource, and as he began to reach his early teens and grow more sensitive to life and people around him, the effect of his father's dedication, his mother's devoutness, the way they cared for others during the war and after, showed in his own deepening conviction and sense of responsibility to others . . . a sense of responsibility to the bitterness and poverty created by the war and to the divisions it had caused even within families like his own!

His father had gone back to Ohio to visit relatives at the end of hostilities and returned home sober-faced and discouraged.

"Their sympathies were Northern," Dr. Wilson told his wife and children. "Many even fought in the Union Army."

The two sides of the family were never very friendly after that.

Tommy's family continued to live in Augusta for five years after the end of the fighting, through the worst years of a military regime that President Johnson had tried to prevent. In the interim election of 1866 so many radical Republicans were elected to Congress that they gained a majority in both Houses. President Johnson struggled to hold the line against vengeance. He vetoed the first Reconstruction Act that divided the South into military districts, but it was passed over his veto, and Augusta's civil administration was replaced by one that was military. Some of the troops were quartered in the First Presbyterian Church.

In 1866, before Tommy was ten, a fourth Wilson child was born, Joseph Ruggles, Jr. Tommy was going on eleven when the news reached Augusta that Jefferson Davis had been released from prison and allowed to join the Confederate refugees in Canada; and he was thirteen, going on fourteen, when General Robert E. Lee passed through Augusta. Young Wilson, burrowing into the crowds that lined the streets to see their hero, managed to get so close that for a moment he stood at Lee's side and looked up into his face. Lee was tall and straight, and every step he took was splendid in spite of his sixty-three years. His hair and beard were silver gray and his face was filled with fine lines.

A few months after General Lee's visit, in the same year of 1870, the Wilson family moved to Columbia, South Carolina, because Dr. Wilson had been appointed as professor in the Presbyterian theological seminary there, as well as pastor of the First Presbyterian Church.

Columbia was only sixty-odd miles from Augusta, but to the sensitive, serious-minded young adolescent it was a shocking other world. The war had hit the heart of this city. General Sherman had marched northward from Savannah to the capital of South Carolina, pillaging, plundering, and burning two thirds of it, and in 1870 it was only partly rebuilt. Large private homes that had once been alive with gracious living now stood silent and empty, others were smoke-blackened shells. Along Main Street there were stray pieces of walls, blocks of rubble, solitary chimneys, and the bridge across the Congaree River was still lacking.

Young Wilson remembered all of his life that moment in early childhood when he heard a passerby say, "There will be war." He hadn't understood it then, but he did now. *This* was war: this ruin, poverty, confusion, waste, hardship, and heartbreak. This was the truth of war.

2. Search for a Vocation

TOMMY WILSON learned something more during the four years that his family lived in Columbia: the futility and waste of vengeance. For in that city and that state occurred some of the worst of Reconstruction.

From the passage of the Reconstruction Act over President Johnson's veto, for several years—until 1877 in South Carolina—the South watched its state debts mount under the corrupt administration of carpetbaggers and scalawags, felt the burden of heavy taxes that went into the pockets of politicians instead of into rebuilding.

President Johnson fought on, but so hostile did relations between him and Congress become that in the spring of 1868 President Johnson was impeached and brought to trial before the United States Senate on charges of high misdemeanor. The radicals failed by one vote to convict him. In the fall General Grant was elected to the Presidency, and the principal plank in the party platform stood for radical Reconstruction.

Grant had been President nearly two years when the Wilsons arrived in Columbia.

Coming to South Carolina's capital they arrived in the heart of the disorder and corruption in government, which meant disorder in everyday life. There were assaults, robberies, race incidents. The Ku-Klux Klan had come into being, and there had been armed clashes between it and the Negro militia.

The housing shortage was acute, and Tommy and his family had to settle in a small house at Pickens and Blandings Streets, near the seminary, but not really large enough for the six of them. The baby Joseph was over three, and his two sisters were adults.

The Columbia of Tommy Wilson's youth is the portion that surrounds the present capitol and the University of South Carolina campus. Gervais Street runs westward through the center of it and down the sweeping hill to the Congaree; and Main Street divides it in a north-south direction. Where Gervais and Main streets cross stands the capitol, and only two blocks away rises the tall steeple of Dr. Wilson's church, one of the buildings that survived General Sherman.

The legislature, meeting in Columbia, contained a majority of Negro members, too few of them educated, most of them being manipulated by unscrupulous whites who had come South to grow rich in this way. With no idea of value, the legislature voted such things as payment of a $450,000 printer's bill. Another time they purchased two hundred cuspidors for themselves at eight dollars apiece. Citizens of Columbia, white or Negro, grown suddenly rich on graft, flaunted themselves about in gaudy clothes and expensive carriages. The governor of the state was a white carpetbagger from Ohio, who had come with the Freedmen's Bureau and won the confidence of the Negroes.

The Wilsons were steadfast folk, and in Columbia lived many others just as steadfast. Life in the state capital was not all misdirected, by any means. The established old families, although impoverished, held to their standards. They sent their children to school if they possibly could, or taught them at home, and they went to church on Sunday. Many of their young people were students in the seminary where Dr. Wilson taught, and many came to the First Presbyterian Church where he preached.

Tommy Wilson naturally sought his friendships among them, and because he was so likable and so thoughtful new friendships were quickly made: with John William Leckie, who was just about his age, and with Francis John Brooke, nearly nine years Tommy's senior, who had come from Richmond, Virginia, to study for the ministry.

While Tommy was adjusting to life in Columbia and making new friends, his parents bought a plot of land on Hampton Street at Henderson, still near the seminary. They were able to build an ample home for themselves, because Jessie Wilson had inherited some money from a relative. It is a two-story, white frame house with a wide front porch, and the interior that Mrs. Wilson designed is very like the house in Staunton where Tommy was born. There is a wide central hall with a stairway, and two rooms on either side of it. Since there was no plumbing or central heating then, each room had its fireplace, water came from a well, and the kitchen was in the basement.

Across the street was the home of the scholarly Charles H. Barnwell. Impoverished by the war, he had opened a private school for boys in a small building behind his house. There Tommy Wilson resumed his education. He was accustomed by now to the routines and disciplines of a classroom, and he found Mr. Barnwell likable and listened with deep interest when the headmaster talked of his own student days at the University of Virginia and the University of South Carolina, right in Columbia.

And young Wilson—too thin, rather sharp-featured, his gentle gray eyes hidden by spectacles—appealed to Barnwell. The lad was mature for his years, trained to be spontaneously helpful. The overworked teacher sometimes asked him to coach the smaller boys.

In his early teens Wilson was the kind of person to whom other students, as well as his teacher, could turn. He possessed a positive sense of right and wrong, a certain quiet confidence, that he conveyed to others. His manner was growing increasingly quiet and serious. He could be gay and full of fun, and his good tenor voice helped his popularity, but his love of studies developed in him the habit of withdrawing to some solitary spot to read.

He never really caught fire from Barnwell's teaching, because his two best teachers were always his father and himself. It was his father who taught him to express his thoughts clearly and precisely.

"Write down your ideas," the older man would advise. "Say exactly what you mean."

His father trained him to have beautiful diction, because being able to speak well in public was the mark of an educated man.

"Learn to think on your feet. Make your mind like a needle, of one eye and a single point. Shoot your words straight at the target. Don't mumble and fumble."

And from his father he learned to absorb and digest a book, not merely to read it.

"The mind is not a prolix gut to be stuffed," said his father. "It is a digestive organ, it is an assimilating organ, and what it does not assimilate it rejects and gets no profit from."

Together they read and discussed and digested the works of Charles Lamb, Charles Dickens, Sir Walter Scott, Daniel Webster, books on American and British history. Because he learned to love books while he was young, Tommy was his own teacher for the rest of his life, and he could apply himself to learning any subject that concerned him. His father gave him a key to the seminary library, and he disappeared into the little building for hours at a time.

He read everything, from the most serious theological matter to adventure stories. Fiction stimulated his imagination in a special way, and he began to spin out his own adventures, with seafaring greatly emphasized. There was small-craft navigation on the Congaree, but he could fancy himself as nothing less than admiral of a fleet in the United States Navy assigned to hunt down pirates. For this he had to learn every kind of ship and every part of a ship and its function. As soon as Admiral Wilson had captured his pirates and rid the sea-lanes of the menace, he wrote a meticulous report to his government of the mission accomplished.

In his voluminous reading in American and British history he discovered a political hero in William Gladstone, Prime Minister of Great Britain. Gladstone was one of the political giants of the age, and he had been prominent in English politics since the age of twenty-three, when he was first elected to the House of Commons, nearly a quarter of a century before Thomas Woodrow Wilson was born. Gladstone was a stern, righteous Scot of the same Covenanter strain as the Woodrows and Wilsons, and as a young man he had seriously considered the ministry instead of public office. He was a humanitarian and a liberal, rising in the meetings of Parliament to speak with eloquence and passion for home rule in Ireland, economy in government, reforms to extend the franchise to workingmen and people in rural areas, reforms in taxation and education.

All the while Tommy Wilson prepared for college with Barnwell and his father, and with American history teeming about him in the streets of Columbia, he followed the stormy career of William Gladstone. He even hung a picture of the large-nosed, roughhewn man in his room.

Gladstone's youthful indecision about his career struck a deep, responsive chord in Wilson, because he could not resolve his own ambitions. His father would surely like him to be a minister, and Brooke was going into the ministry. But Gladstone made the thought of public office appealing. Or would he perhaps go into teaching? Leckie was planning to teach. All Wilson was sure of was that he wanted some kind of academic or scholarly work.

He envied the confidence of Francis John Brooke whose calling was as clear to him as the palm of his own hand. Brooke *knew* he was going to be a Presbyterian minister, and so ardent was his faith that he could not wait to be ordained. He was already preaching. Every time he recited in class he preached. He must tell anyone who would listen of his marvelous message, and a spontaneous congregation came to his rooms in the seminary to hear him, young Wilson among them. The congregation expanded until it had to be moved to the school chapel.

Under the inspiration of Brooke's friendship Wilson's faith, which had always been positive and secure, became compelling. He and Brooke talked and talked of religious matters, although they never really argued, because their views were the same.

"So far as religion is concerned, argument is adjourned," Wilson once said.

But it was Brooke's zeal, his ardor, the contagiousness of his faith that turned the tide for Tommy Wilson, and under Brooke's influence he made a major decision: to join the church.

"It is my religious turning," he concluded.

In a family where there were ministers on both sides of the family for generations back, this was a joyful decision. His father, his mother, his grown sisters, even his seven-year-old brother glowed with happy approval. On the Sunday morning that Dr. Wilson received his own son into membership, Tommy had never felt more loved nor more united with the handsome, dedicated man in the pulpit. After the service he hugged every member of his family.

The boy's career and the rest of his formal education must still be planned, and he and his father held long earnest conferences about it. Very recently the president of the College of New Jersey at Princeton, the Reverend James McCosh, had stopped at the Wilson home on a trip through the region. A graduate of Scottish universities, he spoke with a heavy burr, and he talked glowingly of the New Jersey college, founded by the Presbyterian Church, where Tommy could attend with tuition free as a minister's son. Dr.

Wilson, by now high in the ranks of the church, had studied at Princeton himself, but he knew of several such colleges.

Many Southern colleges had been closed during the Civil War, and funds had not yet been found to reopen them; but near Charlotte, North Carolina, was the small but excellent—and Presbyterian—Davidson College. Tommy and his father decided finally upon Davidson, and to his joy both Leckie and Brooke enrolled with him in the fall of 1873.

Tommy Wilson's decision plunged him into a series of new trials and experiences, and one of the most trying was this first separation from his family. The hubbub and whirl of planning and packing sustained them all for a while, but it was an overbrave group that stood on the gravel platform of the little railway station to see Thomas Woodrow Wilson off to college.

There was no more to do when the train came in but to kiss each one, leap aboard, disappear inside, and look at them through the train window. Seeing them down there on the ground, in a tight little group, as though they were standing as closely as possible for moral support, made Tommy Wilson feel like the small boy who had once clung to his mother's skirts. Jessie Wilson was still lovely and young at forty-seven, and Joseph Wilson at fifty-one stood stalwart, self-contained, regal. Father, teacher, friend, mentor-for-life! Oh, he'd write to them. He'd write, write, write . . .

Wilson and his companions leaned back against the

plush-covered seats to take their slow baptism of soft-coal soot as the recently restored railway puffed and halted and panted its way for nearly a hundred miles to Charlotte. From Charlotte they took the still more recently rebuilt Atlantic, Tennessee and Ohio the last twenty-odd miles to Davidson.

The red brick buildings of Davidson, buried in luxuriant old oaks and elms, comprised about a quarter of the present campus. There was one quadrangle then, and to the east of it a large imposing building called Chambers Hall, named for a benefactor of the college. Of that original quad Eumenean Hall and Philanthropic Hall still stand facing each other, fronted by heavy white columns; and two rows of one-story dormitories called Oak Row and Elm Row. The old chapel of Wilson's day, which stood at the north end of the quad, is no longer there, and the original Chambers Hall, center of life on the campus, burned to the ground many years later and was replaced by a new building.

The central portion of Chambers contained the classrooms, laboratories, and a big unheated auditorium on the second floor, and its two wings were dormitories. Tommy Wilson and John Leckie roomed together in Number 13, on the first floor of the north wing of Chambers.

Wilson had as many comforts as he knew at home, except that he had to do all of the chores himself. Light was from a kerosene lamp that he must clean and fill. His water for washing he must bring in from the well in the yard. His heat came from a fireplace, and he had to cut and carry his own firewood.

His sense of humor and his ingenuity came to his rescue. A Highland fling warmed a fellow up when the fireplace did not, and by shrewd planning he could remain under the warm covers until the last possible second in the morning, when he heard the chapel bell for breakfast. Then—out of bed, wash, into his clothes, dogtrot across the lawn, and drop into his seat before the bell had stopped ringing, joshing late arrivals. John Leckie often shook his head; he could not begin the day with so much sparkle.

The grief of parting with his family vanished quickly as Tommy plunged into campus life. He was one of thirty freshmen, and his excellent singing voice and love of sports won him a quick acceptance. He was underweight and growing rapidly, having almost reached his full five feet ten inches, and so he had to drive himself hard to play a good game of baseball.

He drove himself harder in his studies. In spite of the fine preparation his father had given him, there were gaps in his qualifications, and he was on probation in mathematics and Greek. The freshman-year course at Davidson included Bible, Fowler's English grammar, Gildersleeve's Latin grammar, Hadley's Greek grammar, Towne's algebra, and Pierce's geometry, and before the end of the first term Wilson had shed his probation.

His speaking ability and his talent for expressing himself clearly soon gained him the much coveted election to the Eumenean Society, a literary and debating group that met on the second floor of Eumenean Hall. Here he found something like the intellectual stimulation that his father gave him, and the excitement of those first months of campus life spiraled upward and rushed him along with it as he matched debating and writing talents with upperclassmen. Davidson was in the South; most of its hundred-odd students were Southerners. The terrors of Reconstruction in North Carolina had ended only three years earlier, when the state turned the tide in the election of 1870, and the confiscating, self-seeking, brutal governor, W. W. Holden, had been impeached. Thus, when the Eumenean Society met to hold a formal debate on such subjects as "Was John Wilkes Booth a patriot?" or "Was the death of Lincoln beneficial to the South?" they brought a great deal of passionate oratory to it.

To Wilson the idea of a debating society was a special kind of discovery, one that gave him so much he felt deeply compelled to return the gift with service, whatever service was needed, from serving on the committee that tended the stove in the middle of the room to rewriting the society's constitution.

He overexpended himself so much during that first college experience that the sudden ending of activities in June left him in a state of exhaustion and near collapse. The tedious train ride seemed a thousand miles longer than it had coming northward. When he finally reached his home in Columbia, he had to take to his bed.

Slowly his strength returned, and he and his father were soon deep in conversation about events in Columbia. Dr. Wilson was up to his ears in a controversy with the churchmen who had decided to engage another pastor for the church, so that Dr. Wilson would have only his teaching at the seminary. Dr. Wilson's vanity had been deeply hurt. He felt no overburdening of his abilities by being both teacher and pastor. But his congregation felt otherwise, and they wanted more attention and care from their clergyman.

All through the summer of 1874 the Wilson family was embroiled in the dispute. Dr. Wilson declared that he would not permit the seminary students to go to the First Presbyterian Church but would keep them for services in the school's chapel. A group of students protested, and the controversy became a "case" to be heard by the church's General Assembly. At last Dr. Wilson resigned from his teaching post and accepted an assignment as minister in Wilmington, North Carolina.

Once more—in the autumn of 1874—the family packed up and moved to another home.

Wilmington, thirty miles up the Cape Fear River, was a port for ocean-going vessels, one of the major seaports of the Confederacy. Its harbor bristled with tall masts and stimulated anew Tommy Wilson's love of ships. On its docks stood huge piles of cotton waiting to be loaded, and all along the waterfront lounged seamen and longshoremen, full of adventurous tales and songs.

Tommy was not well enough to go back to college, but he could make friends with the seamen, sometimes going aboard an outbound vessel and returning in the pilot boat.

During his months in Wilmington Tommy roved on a bicycle his father had given him, spent as much time in the open air as possible, trying to regain his health, found a sand-lot baseball team to play with, and tried to keep up with his studies under his father's supervision. Quieted by his infirmity, by the loss of Brooke's and Leckie's companionship, he turned in on himself, and reading hours became escape hours. He taught himself shorthand. His heart and mind were ambitious to do great things, accomplish mountains of work, but his tired frame held him back.

"He seems like an old young man," said the Wilson's Negro servant, as he waited quietly upon Tommy.

Both of his parents felt that he ought to begin to show some interest in girls, but when his mother asked him about it he merely shrugged his shoulders and said, "I really don't know any girls who are intelligent enough to hold a conversation with."

He and his father were making long-range plans to enroll him in college at Princeton. Before the war the

College of New Jersey had been popular with Southerners because of its high scholastic standards. Even though it was Northern now in a new and sensitive way, Southerners were beginning to enroll there again, because of its high scholastic standards and because of the fact that so many Southern colleges had not yet been able to reopen.

To Tommy going anywhere to be educated meant leaving the warmth, closeness, and health-restoring love of his family. He could not have stood the loneliness and idleness of this year of convalescence but for his family. They were all adults now—except for his nine-year-old brother—sharing confidences and judgment, supporting one another through trials and difficulties.

But he was almost nineteen, and he knew he could not cling to the protection of his family forever, any more than he could have gone on clinging to his mother as a small boy. He must step outside of this circle of happiness, and he must step outside of the South, where everyone understood the Southern point of view and what the South had suffered, and venture into the North, where he had never been before.

3. A Southerner in the North

THE journey from Wilmington to the village of Princeton was about five hundred miles—a long tedious distance in 1875—giving a man ample time to think. When at last Thomas Woodrow Wilson walked down Nassau Street, carrying his clothes in his father's duffel bag, searching for his boardinghouse, he attracted little attention. Dozens of other freshmen were doing the same, looking as awkward, overgrown, and underweight as he, some going through the same phase of poor complexion.

"Your room is on the second floor," said his landlady as she labored up the stairs ahead of him.

The hubbub of other arrivals told him he would have plenty of young company, all freshmen who had not yet been asked to join a residence club. Suddenly in the midst of so many strangers, a wave of shyness rendered him helpless momentarily, but as he saw the confusion and homesickness of young men away from home for the first time, confronted by their first campus experience, he felt compelled to extend comfort to others. He had already made his adjustment at Davidson.

As soon as possible he hurried out and down Nassau Street to see the campus. There was old Nassau Hall, surrounded by a sweep of green lawn, where the Continental Congress had once met. Behind it stood two gleaming white Greek temples, Whig Hall and Clio Hall, the debating societies. Off to the right stood the First Presbyterian Church. To the left of Nassau Hall was the eight-sided Chancellor Green Library. This he must see at once!

He vaulted up the stairs, two at a time, to the big reading room and gazed about him. He had never been in so large a library before. A student could lose himself here. Like a man sitting down to an endless dinner, he could try to eat everything in sight. He could stuff himself like a prolix gut. Oh, he must be careful . . . careful . . . choosing his volumes . . . selecting his subjects one by one . . . and digest . . .

He melted quickly into the life of the campus, and his tenor voice found him an early membership in the college glee club. And there was pure joy in going to football and baseball games, and going mad with shouting and cheering. He cast frequent glances at the debating halls, and before the end of his freshman year he was in Whig. He was an able speaker by now, studying the speeches of Edmund Burke, learning to argue and persuade and convince without anger. It wasn't too hard, except when the question of the South was raised; then passions were bound to rise. The compassionate Wilson struggled to explain. These Northern lads didn't *know!* They simply did not know!

There were moments when he discovered that there was much he must learn about the North, such as the time that he lifted his head suddenly on hearing a contagious song.

"What song is that?" he asked.

"That is 'The Star Spangled Banner,' Wilson. Hadn't you heard it before?" He shook his head.

Wilson began to love the College of New Jersey in a way he had not felt about Davidson, partly because he was more mature, partly because there was so much at Princeton to challenge him, a greater diversity of viewpoints, closer contact with what was going on all over the United States and in the world. Dr. McCosh, who struck fear in freshmen as he strode across the campus, was the dynamic heart of the matter. Tommy Wilson took a deep personal pride in remembering the friendship between his father and Dr. McCosh.

Once more young Wilson was caught up in the excitement of campus life and studies, overtaxing his strength, making every free moment count—in the library, in classes listening to brilliant men, in study, in hash sessions with crowds of students after hours. Together they fought the Civil War again and again; they debated the merits of the Republican Party and

President Grant. To the Southerners "Republican" was a hated word because it meant Reconstruction. But there was a Presidential election coming up next year. The tide would turn in '76! Nonsense! declared the Northern students. This was a Republican era. Humph! responded the Democrats.

In world affairs Gladstone was still high in Wilson's esteem even though he had lost an election and been forced to resign as Prime Minister, replaced by Disraeli. Gladstone was a supreme parliamentarian, a splendid and skilled debater, and it was in debate, informed, reasoning debate, that a man's mind came alive.

The pull of politics on his soul grew stronger and stronger. When he expressed himself best on paper—the clearest thoughts in the least number of words—he wrote on politics. When he spoke in debate or in class, he was most eloquent on politics.

By the time he returned to Wilmington after his first year at Princeton, he confessed to his father that his vocation was still not clear, but he was beginning to realize that statecraft of some sort—a seat in the legislature or even Congress—was more attractive than the ministry. He loved his father and knew this was inflicting a hurt on the older man, but his father also loved him and swallowed his disappointment.

In the fall of Wilson's sophomore year the Princeton campus was alive with the excitement of the coming election. Clusters of young men stood on the grounds, arguing and protesting. The debating clubs and informal groups in residence halls were never done arguing.

For the South there was great hope in this national election. General Grant was through! The Republicans had nominated Rutherford B. Hayes of Ohio. The Democratic Party had nominated Samuel J. Tilden, Governor of New York, who had supported Andrew Johnson's compassionate policies, was opposed to corruption and privilege, and admired Thomas Jefferson's ideals.

Now that he had begun to have a sense of his own vocation, Wilson could plunge into current events of the fall of 1876 with joy and relish. Tilden could win! Straw votes said he would. A tide of victory was gathering.

The predictions were accurate. Tilden won the popular vote by some 250,000 over Hayes, but he lost the Electoral College by one vote. A controversy burst forth, centering on the results in Louisiana, South Carolina, Florida, and Oregon. Leaders of each party claimed these states for themselves, accusing the other party of corruption. A special electoral commission was appointed to make an investigation. The results of the investigation, to this day disputed by scholars, declared Hayes elected.

Must the South revolt again? Oratorical young men like Wilson produced volumes of dispute and debate and dire predictions for America's future. But gradually they found that their alarm had been exaggerated, and that President Hayes was as eager to bring an end to Reconstruction as they. He soon withdrew federal troops from the South.

"The stage was cleared for the creation of a new nation," Wilson wrote of it years later.

Politics! Democratic processes! Statecraft! Here and abroad! This must be his life. He must read—and digest—all the history for it that he could. He read through every volume of John Richard Green's *Short History of the English People,* and it touched off a new daydream: his own *History of the American People.* He had already shown a decided flair for writing, and so there was no reason why in a few years he could not attempt such a project.

His daydreams were maturing as he matured. There were no more childish fancies about being an admiral. Now, in his mind's eye, he was America's official historian, and perhaps an officeholder as well.

"Thomas Woodrow Wilson, Senator from Virginia," he wrote on a piece of paper and sat studying it for a long while. The words looked well, and they would sound really fine being announced to a formal gathering.

He was quite unaware that his person and manner were growing quite senatorial. There was more and more in his mien of his father's pulpit dignity. Whether he was harmonizing late at night with fellow students or arguing for low tariffs before the Whig

Society, he was becoming more and more the stalwart, upright, confident senator, or governor, or minister, or teacher, with a gift of being able to impart both wisdom and leadership that others were willing to accept.

He had moved from the beginners' boardinghouse to rooms on the second floor of Witherspoon Hall, a newly opened dormitory, and in his junior year he was elected to membership in a residence club, "The Alligators."

By the time he reached his junior year, Wilson had become one of the most outstanding students at Princeton, respected for his scholarship, his speaking ability, his writing, his religious devotion, and his integrity. His articles had appeared in such college publications as the *Princetonian,* and in November of his junior year he published a well turned essay in the *Nassau Literary Magazine,* "Prince Bismarck." In his senior year he was managing editor of the *Princetonian,* and he wrote another article, "Cabinet Government in the United States," that he sold to a commercial magazine, the *International Review,* of which Henry Cabot Lodge was an editor. Being able to meet the requirements of a professional magazine was all the encouragement an aspiring writer could possibly need. The check that came in the mail was the first money he had ever earned, and he had earned it with his own writing. This money must be spent for something significant! Wilson—now signing his name

"Thomas W. Wilson"—purchased a large bookcase fronted with a pair of glass doors.

During his last weeks at Princeton his friends and companions had an opportunity to measure the real depth of his convictions. One of the big events of graduation week was a debate between the Whig Society and Clio. Wilson and some of his closest friends, such as Robert Bridges, were members of Whig, and with both Wilson and Bridges on their team Whig had an excellent chance of winning.

The subject for the debate was already known: "Free Trade versus a Tariff for Protection." The young men came teeming into the meeting room to draw lots to determine which side of the question they were to support.

Tariff and world trade were subjects that Wilson had done a great deal of reading and thinking about.

"I am really ready for this," was his happy attitude, as he sat laughing and chatting with other members of Whig.

But when the drawing had been made and he heard that his team would be supporting high tariff, his manner turned serious. Without hesitation Wilson stood up and said, "I am in favor of free trade. I cannot argue against my convictions."

A wave of protest rose around him.

"Oh, see here, Wilson! It's just a debate. You know the rules."

"If I were to speak ideas in which I do not believe,

my arguments would have neither force nor sincerity," he told them.

There was no altering him. The debate was held without him, and while two Whig members, one of them Robert Bridges, received prizes for their debating ability, the Whig team did not win.

There were many mixed feelings among his classmates about what Wilson had done. Like the small boy who, thinking he had committed murder, said, "It wasn't an accident. I killed her," he again expressed the truth as he saw it. In the long run those closest to him remembered he had given up a coveted prize himself, and they respected him for it.

"There was a certain integrity in his ideal from boy to man that gave his friends a peculiar confidence in his ultimate destiny as a leader of men," Robert Bridges wrote about it later.

Wilson was a man who usually kept his friends. Even though Leckie and Brooke were not at Princeton with him, he had kept in touch with Leckie until his death two years before, and he still corresponded with Brooke. Robert Bridges would always remain his friend, and so would others in his close Princetonian circle.

Feelings healed before graduation. On the evening of Class Day he stood with his class on the steps of Old Nassau, and they sang their college songs together one more time, while thousands of alumni and visitors strolled about the lawns or sat under the big old trees listening. At graduation he stood thirty-eighth in a class of 107 with an average grade of 90.3, and he had been chosen to give an address. He spoke on the subject, "Our Kinship with England."

The kinship between England and the United States was too deep in the history of both countries ever to be lost, and Wilson's kinship with Princeton was also destined to last.

4. A Southerner in the South

His four years at Princeton brought his vocation as a public officeholder into focus, but Wilson realized full well that he must find some other means of earning a living. His family realized it too, hoping that in time some profession would draw him away from his political interests. They listened patiently while he pointed out that trustworthy officials were essential to a free society, but they hoped for the best, nevertheless.

By the time Tommy returned to Wilmington after his graduation, he had decided that law was the most likely doorway to politics. As he explained this decision to his parents and watched them strive to understand his point of view, forget their own disappointment, allow him to determine the course of his own life, his love for them had never been deeper. Yes, they would send him to law school.

The finest law courses at that time were being offered by the University of Virginia, and in the fall of

1879 Wilson set out for Charlottesville to enroll as a graduate student.

The campus of the University of Virginia, designed and created by Thomas Jefferson, was one of the loveliest that Wilson had ever seen. At one end of a green lawn quadrangle stood the most prominent building, the Rotunda, its top a dome, its front flanked by six massive Grecian columns. Down each side of the quadrangle stretched rows of red brick, white trimmed residence halls, alternately one and two story, the one-storied for students, the two-storied for faculty. Behind them on each side stretched a second row of one-story student rooms. Beyond it all rose the foothills of the forest covered Blue Ridge Mountains.

Thomas W. Wilson, as he enrolled here (an attorney defending a client in court could not be known by a childhood pet name), had to face once more a whole new campus situation. There were over three hundred students, all of them strangers, seventy-eight registered in the Law School. His room on the West Range, Number 31, not far from the one Edgar Allan Poe had once occupied, had its own running water, but that was the only new comfort. He still had to provide his own wood for the fireplace.

Mr. Jefferson's "academical village" proved rich and stimulating. The weight of Jeffersonianism was everywhere, and the debating society that Wilson hastened to join was called the Jefferson Society.

The law courses were stiff and demanding, and law

proved a thoroughly dull subject. As far as he was concerned it was like having hash for dinner every evening of the year.

"The Law is indeed a hard task-master," he wrote to a Princeton classmate. "I am struggling hopefully but with not over-much courage, through its intricacies, and am swallowing the vast mass of its technicalities with as good a grace and as straight a face as an offended palate will allow. I have, of course, no idea of abandoning this study . . ."

It was his steppingstone, his doorway to another career; he had no intention of giving it up even though he was "most terribly bored by the noble study."

So, while his law study overworked him, he overworked at his extracurricular activities to escape its boredom. He was in the chapel choir and first tenor in an octet. His oratory won him immediate recognition, and the maturity he had achieved during his four years at Princeton, his ability to make forthright decisions, made him automatically a leader of other men.

It happened quite spontaneously at times, this rising to the role of leadership, and a sudden incident touched Wilson off during his first winter at the University of Virginia. The young men of the university were gathering in an excited, shouting indignation meeting—more of a war party than a meeting. There was a circus in town; some of them had gone to see the show, and one of the showmen had shouted at the students that they were "ruffians, scoundrels and blackguards."

"He'll apologize!" was the general shout at the mass meeting.

Suddenly horrified at the possibilities of what might occur if all the men with the traveling show had a pitched battle with the students, Wilson struggled and worked his way to the front of the meeting, holding up his hands as a signal that he wished to speak. He certainly did not look robust enough to stop a small fight, let alone the big melee this was going to be. But as the voices subsided and he began to speak, his listeners forgot his appearance, and felt themselves being carried along by the power and strength of his words. This fellow who never danced, smoked, or drank, who read his Bible threadbare, was urging them not to seek revenge. He was pleading for sound reasoning, not violence, for the conduct of educated and cultured men.

"Gentlemen," Wilson asked in conclusion, "is it worth it?"

The advocates of broken heads knew they had lost, and the riotous attack upon the traveling show never occurred.

Both the faculty and students at Charlottesville were drawn to Woodrow Wilson, just as they had been at Princeton. Wilson was acutely aware that this university had more faculty for the number of students than Princeton, and there was a much closer relationship between the two groups as a result. He liked the experience and remembered it in future years.

His most lasting friendships, though, were with the young men in his own age group, and among them were men who would eventually become known to the whole country. One was Richard E. Byrd of Virginia; another was William Cabell Bruce of Maryland. The closest and most enduring friendship developed between Wilson and Richard Heath Dabney of Virginia, and though their careers were to separate them their friendship went on to the end of their days. Wilson called Dabney "thou very ass," and Dabney called Wilson an "illimitable idiot."

Woodrow Wilson considered himself a Virginian. Had he not signed himself, and fancied himself, "Senator from Virginia"? There was something particularly distinguished about the label *Virginian* when attached to the name of a man in public office. He'd been born in Virginia, and he had relatives in Virginia, not far away in Staunton. And so the "illimitable idiot," unable to go home for a one-day Christmas holiday, arranged to spend it with his relatives on the other side of the ridge in the Shenandoah Valley.

The Staunton relatives were Woodrows. His Aunt Marion and Uncle James Bones had moved there from Augusta. Several of his cousins were students at the Augusta Female Seminary in Staunton that was now conducted in the church where his father had preached. He could recall one of them, Harriet Woodrow, or "Hattie," daughter of Uncle Thomas and Aunt Helen Woodrow of Chillicothe, Ohio, because she had paid his family a visit in Wilmington two years before. He hadn't really seen any of the others in so long that so far as he could remember they were all children.

The twenty-three-year-old "Senator" Wilson who arrived at his aunt's house was handsomer than he knew. The sharpness of his features had become lines of strength; his high forehead, Scottish cheekbones, firm chin, and candid eyes bespoke his depth of character. His hair that had been rather sandy as a child was now dark, and he was experimenting with side whiskers to make himself look older for the practice of law. He hoped his cousins wouldn't find him too old.

But there were no children waiting for him in Staunton. Instead he was surrounded by a bevy of beautiful, chattering, perfumed, and beruffled young ladies, and in the happy confusion he bogged down in the worst attack of shyness that he had had in years.

"Oh, do take Tommy in tow!" and they swept him into their celebrations, their house parties, their concerts and recitals and song fests at the Seminary and the Presbyterian Church.

Hattie Woodrow, the young cousin whom he thought he remembered, was staying with the Boneses while she studied at the Seminary. She burst upon him, blooming as the most talented belle of Staunton. She sang; she played the piano and organ; she spoke French. She had lovely, soft brown, curly hair and deep blue eyes. She was as devout a churchgoer as a righteous young man could ever hope to meet.

His Christmas holiday was supposed to be only the day, but he decided to remain a week. Hattie decided that she needed a week too. Could he come to Staunton week ends during the rest of the year? He was sure that he could!

During that precious week Tommy Wilson attended Hattie's recitals, escorted her to parties, only to watch her whirl around the dance floor in the arms of other young men who knew how to dance. He was falling in love! He knew that he was! There was no use trying to remember that he and Hattie were first cousins. There was just no use. He was a grown man, and he had met the girl he wanted to marry.

Thereafter, every week end that he could manage it, he boarded the train for Staunton. He and Hattie went sleighing when there was enough snow, they had long talks about everything that mattered, and between his visits they exchanged letters. They had so many mutual ideas! She earnestly agreed with him that there should be no concerts on the Sabbath. They both liked to sing, especially hymns.

The trips to Staunton were being added to an already overtaxing schedule, but his new ardor carried him along, adding zest to his studies and color to his speeches when he debated before the Jefferson Society.

By now he was such an able speaker that outsiders came to the auditorium to hear him; and, when the announcement was made that Thomas W. Wilson would speak on John Bright before the Jefferson Society in March, 1880, the community of Charlottesville showed so much interest in the program that even ladies were admitted.

John Bright was a prominent English statesman of the time, a fiery champion of the workingman and of free trade, a liberal, another political idol of Wilson's. Fired by both love and hero worship, Wilson rose to new oratorical heights that evening. All of his father's teaching was bearing fruit. His diction was clear, his command of English brilliant and forthright, his meanings precise, his treatment of the subject scrupulously honest.

If John Bright had disapproved of the Confederacy, Thomas W. Wilson must include this.

"I yield to no one precedence in love for the South. But *because* I love the South, I rejoice in the failure of the Confederacy. . . . To the seaports of her northern neighbor the Southern Confederacy could have offered no equals; with her industries she could have maintained no rivalry. . . . The perpetuation of slavery would, beyond all question, have wrecked our agricultural and commercial interests . . ."

In Wilson's description of John Bright's personality, there was a remarkable prophecy of his own: "He has attained to honored age, absolutely without deviation from the principles of his youth. . . . I suppose that it is Mr. Bright's supreme self-restraint that is the chief charm of his delivery. The broad and silent river is more suggestive of power than the hurrying, noisy mountain stream . . ."

He spoke of Mr. Bright's "untiring study" and diction. "Absolute identity with one's cause is the first and great condition of successful leadership." The great lesson in John Bright's life is "that duty lies wheresoever truth directs us."

The room resounded with applause when he finished, and the press covered the event. His speech was printed in the *University of Virginia Magazine*.

He must continue speaking and writing! He must keep himself in the public eye if he was ever to achieve public office. And in a month he had an article published in the same magazine, "Mr. Gladstone, A Character Sketch." As a matter of fact that issue of the magazine carried two Wilson items, the second his April speech before the society, when he and his friend William Cabell Bruce debated one another. Bruce enjoyed just as much local fame as an orator as did Wilson, and the crowd for this affair was even larger.

"Is the Roman Catholic element in the United States a menace to American institutions?" was the subject taken by the two young Presbyterians, and

Wilson spoke for the negative. He gave a stirring plea for tolerance without fear. There was no menace in Catholicism "as a policy," he declared. "Our liberties are safe until the memories and experiences of the past are blotted out and the *Mayflower* with its band of pilgrims forgotten; until our public school system has fallen into decay and the nation into ignorance; until legislators have resigned their functions to ecclesiastical powers and their prerogatives to priests."

Both he and Bruce did so well that the judges were unable to decide which speaker should receive the medal, and many weeks later they gave each a medal, calling Wilson "the best orator" and Bruce "the best debater."

After the meeting Wilson discovered that his Uncle James had come from Staunton to hear him speak. Then, Uncle James could be counted on to give Hattie a report on his latest success, and he'd give her his own most secret and happy thoughts of it the next time he was in Staunton. And he'd tell her that he was now president of the Jefferson Society, sitting in conference with its other officers to rewrite its constitution. He felt very deeply that it was impossible to exaggerate the importance of the legal document upon which an organization or a movement was founded.

When school closed for the summer, Wilson returned to Wilmington and Hattie to Chillicothe, Ohio. She would not be coming back to the Seminary in Staunton in the fall, because she was to begin studies at the College of Music in Cincinnati.

To his whole family Wilson wore his heart on his sleeve. He had already been writing to his parents with complete candor about his love for Hattie. He wanted them to understand, to become accustomed to the idea, to consent in their hearts to his marriage to a first cousin. When he reached Wilmington, he found that once more they were giving their consent to something of which they did not approve and giving it with their usual heroic understanding.

He returned to Charlottesville in the fall, filled with hope, and to his courtship, his law study, and all of his campus activities was added the excitement of a Presidential campaign.

He and other staunch Democrats predicted a "great change of weather" in the coming election. It was time, more than time, for a change, an end of this so-called Republican Era. The young men at the University of Virginia were willing to spend as much passion and energy on the campaign as he.

The Republican Party that had come into its own with Abraham Lincoln was still known as Lincoln's Party. It had saved the Union, it had freed the slaves, it had brought back prosperity, declared its campaign speakers. The Democratic Party was called the party of slave-owning and disunion, and it was genuinely handicapped because it had lost some of its finest leaders, Southern statesmen who had been disfranchised by their participation in the War of the Rebellion. The Republicans campaigned for high tariffs, claiming that lowering them would be bad for business; the Democrats came out for low tariffs and states' rights.

But the Republicans were using the same slogans that they had been using for more than ten years, and the effect was growing a little stale. Tilden's plurality four years ago had proved that. The current Republican candidates, James A. Garfield of Ohio and Chester A. Arthur of New York, won by a very slim margin in the popular vote, and only squeaked into office because they had carried New York and one or two other states with big electoral votes.

"Things are rapidly ripening for a radical change which will soon be imperatively demanded," declared young Wilson.

Perhaps one generation of Southern leaders had been lost, but a new generation was coming along to take its place!

Wilson was growing overtense and overtired, and even after Election Day he could not seem to stop driving himself. The winter was proving a severe one, with snow well ahead of the Christmas holidays. At last a heavy cold settled in Wilson's chest, and he did not have the reserve strength to throw it off. He was too ill to appear for his January examinations.

Was this to be the end of his ambitions? Was ill health to be the stumbling block to his future?

"How can a man with a weak body ever arrive anywhere?" he asked as he tossed his head on the pillow, and fever, aching bones, and a stuffy head dragged him down into despair.

When he was able to move about, he returned home to Wilmington, and there the family doctor declared that his whole digestive system showed signs of abuse—poor food, tension, overwork—and must be slowly coaxed back to health or he would suffer from the permanent ill health that he feared.

It had to be faced, and he and his father decided that he would complete his law studies at home.

Since he was perfectly able to discipline himself as a student, his work did not suffer, but his courtship of Hattie did. He could only write her letter after letter, detailed accounts of his activities, declaration after declaration of his love. He loved her so much that he must write "even when I have to write stupidly." He sent her a volume of Longfellow's poems, and her response was gracious, assuring him that Longfellow was her favorite poet.

This was a deeply lonely existence he found himself in. There came a time in a grown man's life when his traditional family relations did not satisfy, when he must forsake parents and kin and go in search of himself.

"I miss you and the other boys . . . more than you would believe, Heath," he wrote to Dabney, his best friend at the University of Virginia, "and when Saturday night comes, I find myself wishing that I could drop in at the Jeffersonian again . . . I am passing a very hum-drum student's life."

Recovery of his health was slow.

"I am still far from feeling complete confidence in my stomach's good behavior," he wrote to Dabney in March.

The task of coaching his young brother in Latin filled up some of his spring days, and not until the summer months was he able to travel as far as Ohio to see Hattie.

She looked lovelier than ever, and more talented; her long hours of practicing and her new instruction had improved her musical skills. She seemed so happy to see him that he became dizzily optimistic, and he began to escort her to the usual round of parties and dances.

But the serious-minded Wilson had grown more serious-minded during his last few months of solitary study at home. Life, the contemplation of his own future life, had become a deep and profound thing to him, not an endless round of going to parties, parties, parties. In the midst of the gaiety of one of them, he grew suddenly weary of the frivolity of it all, and impetuously he took Hattie by the arm.

"Please, walk in the garden with me . . ."

They stepped out into the cool evening air and followed a path among flowering shrubs. There must be a deciding . . . *now!*

With a sudden burst of words he told her how deeply he was in love with her.

"Marry me right away, Hattie!" he begged.

He felt her stiffen a little with hesitation.

"Tommy, we are first cousins."

"That doesn't matter. My parents have given their consent; surely yours will."

But it was her own consent that was needed, and this she did not give.

"I don't love you enough to marry you," she told him with complete candor, and gradually and gently she led him back into the room full of dancing couples.

He could not rejoin the revelers. Instead he left her in the care of others and moved that same night to a hotel room. From there he wrote her a pleading letter to persuade her to change her mind.

"Reconsider the dismissal you gave me tonight. I cannot sleep tonight—so give me the consolation of thinking that there is still one faint hope left to save me from the terror of despair."

There was not a glimmer of hope from Hattie, even in a long last conversation with her the next day, and so the thoughtful young law student with the ever-deepening soul returned home, adding unrequited love to his burdens of loneliness and frail health.

There had to be another whole year of study before he could receive his law degree, and any part of the discouraging outside world that his law studies did not shut out could be excluded by prodigious reading of history and by writing articles. In June, 1882, the University of Virginia sent him his degree of LL.B. *in absentia,* marking the end of a long, dreary part of his life. Now that it was done he could think about what was to come next—if anything really would.

Family conversations about where best to begin practicing law soon led him to discover that, once a man's spirits have reached the bottom, there is only one direction in which they can move, and that is upward. True, he did not feel robust even yet; true, he would need much longer to get over his love for Hattie; true, he had no real sign that he was to make a mark in the world. But just making plans was in itself stimulating.

He wanted to remain in the South, because he was a Southerner, and this was the part of the world he understood best. Well, that point was settled. He and his parents soon agreed that the largest and most vigorous Southern city was Atlanta, Georgia. Atlanta was a bustling hub in the economic wheel of the southeast. The city that Sherman had devastated was now rebuilt and a beehive of business. A wise and logical place to start a law practice!

Another parting from his family, and he could not help but know how difficult it was for his parents. His departure left only sixteen-year-old Joseph at home with them, for both of his sisters had long since married. Marion was Mrs. A. R. Kennedy, living in Mayesville, Kentucky; and Anne was Mrs. George Howe, living in Columbia, South Carolina. He hoped that the stimulation and hubbub of his packing and planning would sustain them for a little while, as it was sustaining him.

Of course, he'd take his favorite bookcase, the one bought with the only money he had ever earned, and a picture of Gladstone. And his mother was making him some fine new shirts. She wanted him to look his best as he represented his clients in court.

When Thomas Woodrow Wilson stepped from the train in Atlanta that same June, he was twenty-five, tall, slim, quite handsome, looking more like a senator than ever. He had brought with him a considerable fund of knowledge, a well-developed capacity for expressing himself on paper or on a speakers' platform, and a heart once more filling with hope.

One thing had been left behind: his first name, especially the "Tommy." Tommy had been a mamma's boy when small, a sickly young man, a rejected suitor. Henceforth, he would sign himself, call himself, and expect to be called Woodrow Wilson.

5. Ellen Axson

ATLANTA was really alive! The humming city made Woodrow Wilson tingle as he set about the task of finding lodgings. As soon as he had rid himself of his luggage, he looked up Edward Renick, a fellow law student now practicing here. Renick could surely set him off in the right direction.

But Renick, it turned out, could give advice in great abundance, and that was about all. He had no law practice and was as dependent upon family support as Wilson.

"You are right about Atlanta's progressiveness," he said jovially. "The city is attracting young lawyers like a magnet. There are more attorneys in Atlanta than any city could possibly need, many of them beginners and willing to work for a pittance to become established."

They chuckled together over the hopeless situation, but Wilson had no intention of changing course, and Renick did not want him to. They would form a law partnership, they agreed, Renick & Wilson, and their complementary personalities and combined legal talents would serve the people of Atlanta and surrounding Georgia as no other law firm could. Over the years they would become the outstanding dignitaries of the profession. If Woodrow Wilson ran for public office and was elected, his law partner could handle the firm's affairs while he was away.

They found themselves office space, one flight up, in the back of 48 Marietta Street, still an important commercial street in downtown Atlanta, and they took living quarters together in the home of a widow on Peach Tree Street.

For Woodrow Wilson life in any community began with worship at the Presbyterian Church on Sunday morning, and in Atlanta it continued with Sunday afternoon strolls with his landlady's niece, Katie Mayrant. The combined zest of a new career in a new city, a new friend, and a new flirtation sent his spirits soaring, and he felt a secret twinge of embarrassment at the speed with which his broken heart was healing.

His friendship with Renick flourished and endured; his interest in Katie Mayrant faded slowly; his law practice never rose much above zero. Was this the profession that he had thought would provide the doorway to public office? Not only was it overpopulated and fiercely competitive in Atlanta, but there was the added problem for a man of scruples of refusing unsavory cases. Wilson's stiff-necked attitude on the type of cases he was willing to handle sometimes rubbed the fur the wrong way on local politicians, who were in a position to direct law business to him. But he could not persuade himself to make a career out of helping rascals to squirm out of their just responsibilities. That was not how he understood the law. The spirit and intent of the law were to serve men, not to injure or enslave them. Wilson and Renick saw eye-to-eye on this point. Their law firm would enjoy a just prestige earned by their integrity over a long period of time.

In fact, there was no conflict between the two young lawyers on anything. They enjoyed the same books, sometimes read aloud together, and then "digested" their reading in long discussions. They shared their friends as well.

A friend of Edward Renick's, Walter Hines Page, appeared on the scene from New York one day. He was a reporter with the New York *World,* assigned to cover the tariff question locally. There was a bill before Congress to revise the existing tariff laws, and the previous spring President Arthur had appointed a commission to investigate the situation. The U. S. Tariff Commission was on its way to Atlanta to hear testimony there, and since Page was a born and bred Southerner this reporting assignment had fallen naturally to his lot.

Renick introduced Page to Wilson, and the three fell to talking.

Page was a North Carolinian, about a year older than Wilson, a fellow intellectual with the problem of uncertain health, a liberal Southerner who shared with Wilson the desire to see the division between North and South healed and hatreds assuaged. His recollections of the Civil War were even more vivid than Wilson's, because Sherman on his northward march through the Carolinas had marched his troops right under the windows of Page's home, and had used the Page home for headquarters. Walter Page could remember watching cavalrymen run their swords through bedding and upholstery, looking for hidden valuables.

"It was a huge army," said Page. "It took all day to file past our house."

They talked about everything, until at last they got around to the tariff question. On this question Woodrow Wilson knew exactly where he stood, and he was extremely well informed.

"The present tariffs are too high. They shut out world trade, and will create resentment and hostilities that could lead to war."

"America cannot exist unto herself."

"Our industries don't need as much protection as the protectionists claim."

"They would be stronger if they were required to meet natural competition instead of being coddled."

They were in complete agreement, and they excited one another with each added comment.

Page was so impressed with Woodrow Wilson that he said, "Wilson, will you address the commission?" Wilson was delighted with the opportunity to serve the public interest. It would be his first real opportunity to be tested in public debate on a national issue. The members of the commission would not be fellow students, but hardheaded, experienced officeholders, grown callous to oratory. The brief that he prepared must be the finest and soundest piece he had ever written.

When he finally stood before the federal commissioners—not to mention the mayor of Atlanta—he knew in his heart that he was making a deep impression, in spite of his youth, forcing these men to think in terms of general principles, of international relations, making them raise their sights above selfish interests.

He asked them to throw manufacturers "upon their own resources" rather than hold them "in the lap of the government. . . . Such theories discourage skill, because it puts all industries upon an artificial basis."

As soon as he was through, one of the commissioners hurled a question at him: "Are you an advocate of the repeal of all tariff laws?"

"Of all *protective* tariff laws!" Wilson corrected at once.

The limelight, the justification of Page's faith in him, the obvious success of his testimony kept Wilson's pulse racing as he accepted congratulations; and, at last, gathered in his office with Renick, Page, and several other young men, who had followed them back, they talked and talked, agreeing that this day's stimulation to their own thinking must be repeated. Then they would meet again, they decided. The result was that Wilson and his circle formed a local branch of the Free Trade Club of New York, meeting every other week, to discuss the great issues of the day, usually tariff laws. Their pattern for debate was like the British House of Commons, and their mentor was Woodrow Wilson. He was not yet a member of the bar!

A month later, though, he presented himself before the formidable Judge George Hillyer for his bar examination. Judge Hillyer and four other experienced attorneys pounded Wilson with questions for two hours, and he finished with colors flying.

"He was nothing short of brilliant," said Judge Hillyer later.

Wilson had been in Atlanta only since June, and he was already a prominent member of the community. In December he learned that the Tariff Commission had recommended that Congress make large reductions in the tariff rates, and the following spring a bill was enacted effecting five per cent reductions. Five per cent was not nearly enough, but the trend was in the right direction. It made a man feel really alive to realize that he might have exerted some constructive influence to bring about a national trend.

But financially he was still dependent upon his

father for support, because law clients were so few and far between. He was beginning to entertain serious doubts about the wisdom of continuing as a practicing attorney. He devoted his afternoons to writing in the hope of earning some money, but magazines rejected his articles.

He discussed his situation candidly with his friends, and his thinking began to clarify. He was a scholar and he liked politics. Perhaps political science was his field, and perhaps he ought to pursue it by graduate study, with the idea of teaching the subject.

Johns Hopkins University was the only place he could find such courses, and since Page was a Hopkins man he chatted with him about it. Page knew that Johns Hopkins gave a certain number of fellowships in political science, and that the standards were high. Before Johns Hopkins had opened, American students had had to go abroad for their graduate study.

The thought lived on in Wilson's mind. By May he had made his decision to give up law practice.

"My dear Heath," he wrote to Dabney, who was then studying in Germany, "I have about made up my mind to study, at Johns Hopkins University, the very subjects which you are now studying in Germany under the great masters with unpronounceable names . . . I can never be happy unless I am enabled to lead an intellectual life . . . Now, here it is that the whole secret of my new departure lies. You know my passion for original work, you know my love for composition, my keen desire to become a master of philosophical discourse, to become capable and apt in instructing as great a number of persons as possible. My plain necessity, then, is some profession which will afford me a moderate support, favourable conditions for study, and considerable leisure; what better can I be, therefore, than a professor, a lecturer upon subjects whose study most delights me?"

So his thinking was clear at last! He would become a teacher of political subjects.

During the last few weeks in Atlanta, when he and Renick were concluding their partnership, Wilson was actually given the legal affairs of a paying client—his mother. His Uncle James Bones had handled her affairs up to now, but apparently she felt that just at this point her son needed a vote of confidence.

The assignment took Wilson to Rome, Georgia, where his Uncle James was now living, and there he had a chance to visit with the whole family. His cousin Jessie, whom he had once thought he murdered, was married and living nearby.

Rome, like Staunton, Virginia, was built on a cluster of hills in the tip of the Blue Ridge in northwestern Georgia. The business and factory sections, which had been thoroughly burned by General Sherman before he started his attack on Atlanta and his march to the sea, showed little signs of damage now. Rome was a lovely, old, and prosperous town, so typically Southern, with its big white homes of plantation owners, giant oak trees, and—since this was April—its blooming azalea, honeysuckle, and fruit orchards. It certainly wore an atmosphere to put a young man in his twenties into a sentimental and romantic frame of mind.

He was filled with the mood of spring when he went to church on Sunday morning with the Bones family, and there during the service he sat watching the minister's daughter, Miss Ellen Axson.

"What a pretty bright face," he thought. "What splendid, mischievous, laughing eyes! I'll lay a wager that this demure little lady has lots of life and fun in her!"

He did not know that she had already seen him walking by, beneath a window where she was sitting, and had said to a friend, "Who is that fine-looking man?"

Since his father was acquainted with the Reverend S. Edward Axson, Woodrow Wilson must call at the manse at once and convey his father's respects. He called persistently again and again, quickly casting aside the pretense of calling on Ellen's father. He took her walking, took her boating on the Coosa River, talked with her for long hours about books and music and painting. She was the daughter of a cultured and learned home, and particularly gifted as a painter. She had golden brown hair, large brown eyes; and she had that same fragile, Southern-lady quality that his mother had when she moved about with tiny steps in her long, rustling skirts.

They knew in a very few weeks that they were going to be married eventually, but when he talked of giving up his plans to go to Johns Hopkins in order to find some salaried post right away, she proved not fragile at all.

They both had responsibilities, she pointed out, he to himself most of all. He must complete his education, obtain his doctorate, seek the teaching post he wanted, have the leisure he needed for reading and writing, and perhaps some day an elective office. Why not?

As for herself, he could see what her responsibilities were. Her father was a widower, and she was the oldest of four children. Her brother Stockton was in college, her nine-year-old brother Edward was at home, and her sister Margaret was an infant. She was her father's hostess at the manse and Edward's and Margaret's foster mother. She could not plan in haste any more than he.

And so they did not plan in haste, but they did plan with a great deal of help and encouragement from two delighted Southern Presbyterian families. Edward would go to live with an uncle, and an aunt took the infant Margaret. While Woodrow was completing his year of study at Johns Hopkins, his fiancée would go to New York City to study at The Art Students League.

"It is something I dearly want to do," she assured him, "and I shall not disturb you with too much of my company while you are studying."

"You are the most beautiful woman in the world," he assured her.

"And I am betrothed to the greatest man in the world and the best."

Tense, dizzily happy, he prepared to go off to Baltimore. Dabney must be the first to know! As soon as Woodrow Wilson reached Baltimore he began his letter to Heath Dabney: "I am the most complacently happy man in the 'Yewnighted States' . . ." His Ellen, Miss Ellie Lou, "grew up in the best of all schools—for manners, purity, and cultivation—a country parsonage." There followed a thousand reasons why he had fallen in love with her. "Why she fell in love with me must always remain an impenetrable mystery."

Had he ever been in love before? He couldn't have been.

The newly engaged couple kept the postman busy during the winter months. He wrote page after page of his life and studies in Baltimore, about the book he was writing with encouragement from his professors.

Johns Hopkins was in the busy center of Baltimore, on Howard Street near the Peabody Library and the Conservatory of Music, and he had a room on nearby North Charles Street. Walter Page's recommendation, he found, had been modest. The trustees had gathered together the finest and most learned teachers they could find when they created the courses of study at Johns Hopkins. For Woodrow Wilson his course with Professor Herbert Baxter Adams in history was the high point. Professor Adams conducted a round table discussion every Friday evening, and so impressed was he with Wilson's scholarship and ability to study by himself that he released Wilson from assignments and let him go ahead on his own.

Under Professor Adams's direction Wilson began to write his first book, on a phase of American government, starting off with the article, "Committee or Cabinet Government." It appeared in the January, 1884, issue of *Overland Monthly,* an important literary and current-events magazine published in California, and it took some of the sting out of his failure as a lawyer to see himself once more in the public eye. This new direction he was taking toward teaching, lecturing, and writing could very well be a route to public office. He went on to work on more chapters, bringing each one to Professor Adams and the Friday seminar, reading his material to faculty and fellow students, always touching off a brilliant and stimulating discussion.

With his writings and seminars, to which he added glee club, debating society, and literary society, the winter months passed swiftly. There was only one serious disturbance, and that was in Ellen's life. She was called home suddenly by her father's death, and after settling family affairs in Rome she moved to the home of her grandfather, the Reverend I. S. K. Axson in Savannah, before returning to her studies in New York City.

By summertime, when she was back in Savannah and Woodrow was home with his family in Wilmington, there were not many times when Ellen and Woodrow could be together because of the distance, but they could go on writing letters. He was putting the finishing touches on his book, he told her, calling it *Congressional Government*.

"Dear Mother makes pastoral calls," he wrote to Ellen. "I write after breakfast, drive before supper, and after supper generally read aloud while dear Mother sews or embroiders. Between the morning writing and the afternoon driving, I attend to father's business letters and to my own correspondence . . ."

When he and Ellen were married, he determined, their home life would be like this. He intended to be as loving and charming a father as his own father had been and still was, and he would give his children every benefit of his scholarship, his devotion, and a fair share of his time no matter how busy and important he might become. . . .

In the fall he wrote to Ellen from Baltimore, "I have just finished preparing my manuscript to be sent to Boston."

His manuscript had already won him a five hundred dollar fellowship at Johns Hopkins for his second year, but sending it to a commercial publisher was another matter. How many houses would turn it down before one accepted it for publication, if any one ever did?

To his utter amazement the first house to which

he sent it, Houghton, Mifflin & Company, accepted it.

"They have actually offered me as good terms as if I were already a well-known writer!" he wrote ecstatically to Ellen.

The whole world seemed to be turning bright. He had met the woman he was to marry; he had signed a contract for his first book; and that same fall of 1884 the Democratic Party at last broke through and elected Governor Grover Cleveland of New York to the Presidency. A split in the deteriorating Republican Party helped considerably, because many independent Republicans, tired of the reactionary element in their own party, backed the Democratic slate.

Wilson's knowledge of current events was growing keener as he read and wrote and kept in touch with such men as Walter Page of the *World* and Robert Bridges of the *Nation*. Page was an ardent admirer of President Cleveland, who stood for lower tariffs and civil service reform, and was a well read and able lawyer.

Now that Wilson was entitled to consider himself a published author whose opinions could influence readers in every corner of the country, he delved with more passion than ever into keeping up with public affairs. A powerful labor movement was growing. The West was developing rapidly in the hands of families that had migrated out to land grants. Railroads were being built at a tremendous rate.

His second winter at Johns Hopkins moved as

swiftly as the first, because he was looking forward to bound copies of *Congressional Government,* receiving offers of teaching posts, and planning with Ellen for a June wedding in Savannah.

When bound copies did reach him, the first copy went in the mail immediately to his father, the person to whom it was dedicated: "patient guide . . . gracious companion . . . best instructor and most lenient critic . . ."

"My Precious Son," wrote back the aging minister. "Your book has been received and gloated over. The 'dedication' took me by surprise, and never have I felt such a blow of love. Shall I confess it?—I wept and sobbed in the stir of the glad pain. God bless you, my noble child, for such a token of your affection . . ."

The second copy went to Ellen.

Highly favorable reviews began to appear early in 1885. Gamaliel Bradford in the *Nation* called it "one of the most important books, dealing with political subjects, which have ever issued from the American press."

The success of his book—on a political subject—brought into sharp focus once more his deepest ambition: public office. Now that the Democratic Party was back in power for the first time since the Civil War, a liberal Democrat could dare to entertain some hopes for himself.

But he was to be married in a few weeks, and so he

must think of a salaried post at once. As he and Ellen and his family pondered his various offers, the one that seemed most attractive to them came from Bryn Mawr, a brand-new college for women, founded by Quaker interests, planning to hold its first classes in the fall of 1885. Even though he had misgivings about taking a post under a woman dean, Woodrow Wilson realized that a teacher of history could hope for unlimited opportunity to display his talents in a new situation where everyone was striving to create a first-class college and where there were no outmoded traditions to inhibit him.

The salary at Bryn Mawr was to be only $1500, not nearly enough for him and Ellen to live on, but he accepted it with the understanding that he be permitted to give lectures on the outside. And of course there would eventually be royalties on his new book.

Ellen Axson and Woodrow Wilson were married on June 24, 1885, in the parlor of the old manse in Savannah, with both Ellen's grandfather and Woodrow's father officiating. The bride had just turned twenty-five; the groom was twenty-eight. After the service and the reception, Mr. and Mrs. Woodrow Wilson left for a secluded cottage in Arden, North Carolina, for their honeymoon.

In the fall, when they journeyed to Bryn Mawr, Pennsylvania, they would be leaving the South for many years, not to live there again until he had become President of the United States.

6. Bryn Mawr and Wesleyan

BRYN MAWR is today a sophisticated suburb, a short train ride west of Philadelphia. But when Woodrow and Ellen Wilson went there it was rural countryside, and the slow, creaky train went only to within a quarter of a mile of the campus. Since the school was brand new a great deal remained to be done as far as the buildings and lands were concerned. The grounds were not landscaped, and the roads and paths were unpaved. Walking was either muddy or dusty, depending upon the weather.

The school consisted of two buildings: Taylor Hall, where the library and classrooms were, and Marion Hall, which was the student dormitory. The faculty lived in a row of three houses: the Deanery, where the Dean lived, the Scenery, and the Betweenery, where the Wilsons had rooms on the second floor.

They looked at each other in despair when they saw their cramped living space. They were both used to ample homes, and they both liked to have friends for dinner, to have relatives come and visit for weeks at a time in the traditional Southern manner. But they had to accept their situation for the time being, at least until Woodrow could find a way to increase his income. And so, after they had set up his bookcase and her easel, they managed to arrange the rest of their possessions.

There were other adjustments that they both had to make. He had never been in any but a man's college with men students and men faculty members. While the president of Bryn Mawr was a man, Dr. James Rhoads, Woodrow Wilson found that teaching a classroom full of girls brought out his old streak of shyness. He covered it as well as he could with sternness and constraint, and his students thought him cold, humorless, and distant. He was wearing a thick, handle-bar mustache to conceal his youth; and his thinness, sharp features, and rimless glasses completed the effect. While he knew he was giving them full measure of the knowledge they needed, he was not reaching them as a person.

"Some of them take me for a minister," he told Ellen. "I made a joke in class today and they all wrote it down solemnly in their notebooks."

As for Ellen, she was a little taken aback by the Northern women she was meeting at Bryn Mawr, by their bold mentality especially. She was cultured and well educated herself, but she never expected to exercise her education in any way except to find private happiness in it, to be gracious and interesting in her own drawing room, and to be an adequate intellectual companion for her husband. These girls talked frankly of becoming doctors and lawyers! They even wanted to vote! She and Woodrow shared doubts about such advanced education for women.

They accomplished more during their first months at Bryn Mawr than they realized. They became loved and respected by both faculty and students, she for her gentle charm, her devotion to her husband, and her talent as a painter, and he for his able teaching and his sincerity and dedication.

But they both felt isolated from their families and from affairs of the world. He kept up by reading as much as he could, by corresponding with men like Dabney, Bridges, and Page. He had not been able to supplement his salary as much as he had hoped, although he had sold an article to the *Atlantic Monthly*, "Responsible Government under the Constitution." In March he welcomed the chance—arranged by Robert Bridges and others—to speak to a meeting of Princeton alumni in New York City on "The College and the Government."

Ellen was expecting her first child soon, and early in April she went to Gainesville, Georgia, to stay with her Aunt Louisa, Mrs. Warren Wade, who was raising her sister Margaret, now old enough to run and romp. The baby was born on April 16, 1886, a girl named Margaret for Ellen's mother.

"You are being addressed by a father," Woodrow Wilson wrote joyfully to Robert Bridges. "I have a little daughter three days old."

Until Ellen felt well enough to come home, Woodrow Wilson filled up his time by taking a trip to Washington to watch Congress and the Supreme Court in action, and another trip to Boston to see his publishers.

Congressional Government was still selling so well, even being translated into other languages, that they wanted him to write more; and D. C. Heath & Company wanted a textbook on the whole subject of government, its history and development, and the different types of government in the world. He signed this contract eagerly.

His second book contract plus an invitation from Johns Hopkins to give a series of twenty-five lectures to the graduate students for a fee of five hundred dollars meant that during the latter part of their second year at Bryn Mawr the Wilsons could rent a cottage of their own on nearby Gulph Road. Room enough at last for themselves, their tiny daughter, the second child they were expecting, and for guests. Now Ellen's older brother Stockton could come for a visit. They planned that during their third year Mary Hoyt, Ellen's cousin, would stay with them so that she could attend Bryn Mawr.

"It was so like those two to think, as soon as they had anything, of sharing it!" said Mary Hoyt.

When school closed for the summer, Ellen returned to Aunt Louisa's, and her second daughter, Jessie Woodrow Wilson, was born August 28, 1887.

Woodrow Wilson's father came to Bryn Mawr for a long visit, and the aging minister shook his head and smiled at Ellen's industry and ability to make a dollar stretch. She managed all the money, even taking cooking lessons to be able to economize in every way, and made all the children's clothing herself. But he frowned on the fact that the tense and high-strung Woodrow was once more working too hard, and there seemed to be no way of preventing it as long as he was at Bryn Mawr. His teaching responsibilities had increased, but the school could afford neither to give him an increase in salary nor an assistant. He had signed a second three-year agreement on condition that they provide him with an assistant "as soon as possible," but it never quite became possible.

He was growing discontented and frustrated, and Ellen knew it. He was thirty-one, he said to her, and so far he had done nothing with his life.

She did not point out to him that he was writing his second book, that he now had his Ph.D. from Johns Hopkins, and that he was making a very particular mark in the educational field. He was not a man to look back or rest on his laurels. He had too much capacity and imagination to remain in so provincial a place forever. He would always be in search of wider horizons.

And he was a man who loved life, who liked recreation and fun and knew how important they were; but at Bryn Mawr he had neither the time nor the opportunity for relaxation. He could allow himself only an hour's walk in the afternoon, carrying his notebook along and jotting down ideas for his lectures.

"I'm beginning to hate this place very cordially," he confided to Ellen one day; and she did all she could to encourage him to seek a new appointment.

He passed on to his friends the news that he was available for a new post: to his former law partner, Edward Renick; to Heath Dabney, who had returned from Germany and was teaching at the University of Virginia; to Walter Page, now manager and editor of the *Forum;* to Robert Bridges, who had joined the staff of *Scribner's Magazine.*

His availability was good news to several institutions looking for effective teachers, and he received a most attractive offer from Wesleyan University: a professorship in history and political economy at a much higher salary and a chance to teach *men!*

Ellen needed only to see his eagerness to encourage him to accept the post at the Methodist university.

The trustees at Bryn Mawr were deeply chagrined that Dr. Wilson wished to leave, even though they did nothing to make it possible for him to stay.

"It's too late in the season to replace you by fall," he was told; and he retorted, "You have ample time to find someone else."

When they reminded him that he had accepted a second three-year contract, he reminded them that his new contract had called for an assistant and they had given him none. Dr. Wilson showed clearly that he was a stiff-necked, uncompromising fellow when he was convinced that he was in the right.

Perhaps he was testier with the trustees than he might have been another time, but this same spring his mother had died rather suddenly, and he and his father, sisters, and brother felt their grief very deeply indeed. His father had been crushed by the loss, and Woodrow tried to express something of what he felt in a letter to Heath Dabney:

"My first news of her condition was the news of her death. Your letter came while I was away with my poor bereaved father in Tennessee . . . and since I returned I have had work enough to deaden the pain of my loss. . . . My mother was a mother to me in the fullest, sweetest sense of the word, and her loss has left me with a sad, oppressive sense of having somehow suddenly lost my youth. I feel old and responsibility-ridden."

The plan to leave Bryn Mawr and take up a new life in another kind of community gradually restored his spirits. All summer he worked with great concentration on his new textbook, *The State,* to have his desk clear for lesson-planning in the fall.

With deep humility Woodrow and Ellen Wilson hoped that they would be able to make friends in Connecticut.

"I hear that New Englanders are cold and unfriendly," said Ellen.

Woodrow nodded. He'd heard the same thing. They would see.

In the historic, colonial city of Middletown, in the heart of the rich Connecticut River Valley, they found warm and congenial friends at once.

The red sandstone college buildings were on High Street, and their home just across the way at 106 High, a two-story white frame colonial house, was ample enough for a manse. Woodrow Wilson inspected the rooms with frank pleasure. Now his little girls could have the kind of romping space, indoors and out, that he had had as a small child in Staunton and Augusta.

Wesleyan was a small college with only a little over two hundred students and twenty faculty members, but it was old enough to be seasoned and well equipped. It had been founded by the Reverend Dr. Laban Clark and opened in September 1831 with the vigorous and liberal Wilbur Fisk as its president, urging sports for the young men and a forward-looking curriculum, which added courses in modern literature, science, and fine arts to the usual Latin and Greek.

When Wilson joined the faculty nearly sixty years later, he found the same eagerness for progressive ideas in teaching. He very soon began to advocate allowing the students to elect some of their subjects, and the college listened.

"As a matter of fact, Dr. Wilson, we have already had some conferences on the idea of electives."

The school had a most adequate library, and for this Dr. Wilson was deeply grateful. The sports program was pure joy. How long had it been since he had attended a football game!

He became one of the faculty advisers to the Football Association and watched practice as well as games, sometimes mapping out plays for the team.

At the Thanksgiving Day game between Lehigh and Wesleyan, Dr. Wilson sat on the sidelines watching Lehigh make two touchdowns and Wesleyan morale sink lower and lower. Something had to be done, and he must do it.

He jumped up, waving his umbrella in the air like a band leader, and called, "Now is the time to yell!" He kept the students yelling and cheering until Wesleyan made a touchdown. One touchdown led to another, and the game ended in a tie score instead of defeat.

"Who was that fellow?" someone asked.

"Oh! That's Professor Woodrow Wilson, a new man on the Wesleyan faculty."

He was the soul of dignity in his classrooms, but now he could tell a joke or one of his limericks and know that his students would enjoy it with him instead of solemnly writing it down. It was positively refreshing to be teaching young men. Teacher and students could goad one another to think, think, think. He still considered debating the most effective stimulant to a man's mind, provided the debater spoke out of conviction and argued for the side in which he believed. To make certain that his students received the full benefit of debating he organized them into a "Wesleyan House of Commons," a Prime Minister and Cabinet. When the Prime Minister lost a debate in the House of Commons, he and his Cabinet went out of office.

The more Woodrow Wilson taught, thought, debated, read, and wrote, the more lucid his own political viewpoint became. His textbook, *The State,* was completed and to be published in the fall of his second year at Wesleyan. In the process of studying the metamorphosis of the different kinds of government in the world, from the caveman who ruled with a club to the present time, he was beginning to see that the next step for mankind was international government.

"More and more, international conventions have come to recognize in their treaties certain elements of right, of equity, and of comity as settled, as always to be accepted in transactions between nations." But as yet, international law was really not law because it could not be enforced. In many historic instances small states had banded together to form a larger nation for their mutual benefit and protection: the United States was an excellent example of this. Often several nations banded together for safety for a while under a treaty.

Even before the successful appearance of *The State,* Woodrow Wilson's reputation as an historian and political economist was growing, and Harvard asked him to write a book in their series, "Epochs of American History." He was ready for a new book contract and very soon began to write *Division and Reunion,* covering the history of the United States from 1829 to 1889.

He was still lecturing at Johns Hopkins and at nearby Brown University, and he was often asked to be guest speaker at other universities. Wherever he spoke, the hall was full, sometimes crowded, because he was so gifted, so well informed, and he expressed himself so clearly.

He and Ellen were really comfortable now, and extremely happy at Middletown. They enjoyed their home, their friends, their stimulating life, and they did not feel isolated as they had at Bryn Mawr.

Woodrow Wilson could no longer call himself a failure or bemoan the fact that he had done nothing with his life. Wesleyan had changed that. Other universities were noticing him, and when he had been at Wesleyan only a year an offer came from the College of New Jersey through his classmate Robert Bridges to return to his own alma mater. But his covenanting conscience would not allow him to accept the tempting offer.

"My dear Bob," he wrote to Robert Bridges, "I am under no contract obligation to stay here any longer than I choose; but when I came here the department of which I have charge had, in incompetent hands, greatly run down at the time of my election. They wanted it built up; that I have been partially able to do: but, were I to leave it now it would collapse again, for a small college like this has by no means the same chances for obtaining a good or even a tolerable man on short notice that Princeton has . . ."

The autumn of the Wilsons' second year at Wesleyan was a high point. Their third daughter, Eleanor Randolph, was born in October, 1889; they received bound copies of *The State;* and Ellen's brother Stockton arrived to spend the year with them so that he could attend Wesleyan.

Dr. Wilson's own personal growth went on, and long before the end of his second year he was ready for wider horizons.

The college at Princeton repeated its offer, and this time he accepted a post as professor of law and political economy.

He wrote his father a joyous letter about it, and he and Ellen prepared to move their possessions and their three children to New Jersey.

7. Return to Princeton

DR. WOODROW WILSON arrived in Princeton in 1890, a most impressive looking person, clean-shaven by now, more imperial than ever, his rimless glasses clipped firmly to the bridge of his nose, his face stern and solemn until he decided to bless someone with a smile. He brought with him a reputation for being the successful author of books and articles and an inspiring lecturer. With him were his beautiful young wife and three lovely little girls, aged four, three, and almost one.

From the moment that the warmhearted, surprisingly attractive Wilson family arrived at the Nassau Hotel, to wait until their rented house at 72 Library Place was ready, for the next twenty years they were a vital part of the community of Princeton, as well as of the college. They lived generously, sharing themselves and their home, and drew people to them.

They discovered two Presbyterian churches. Part of the congregation of the original church had seceded because of an internal conflict. The man who could remember the Civil War and was writing *Division and Reunion* saw a responsibility here. He and his wife did not join either church when they arrived, but they both hoped that they could bring the two quarreling groups back together eventually.

He was certain in a very few months that he would be at Princeton for a long time. There was so much to be *done* here! The scholastic standards were lax. Entrance exams were too easy. Students cheated to pass their term exams and joked boldly about it. Where was the challenge and discipline? How could a college produce responsible leaders for a nation in this way? Other young members of the faculty shared his indignation, but there was little they could do about it under the present administration.

The man who had been Wilson's father's friend, the dour Scot, James McCosh, had retired, and in his place was Dr. Francis Lindley Patton. Dr. Patton added new buildings to the campus with gusto, but otherwise he was a lazy administrator.

As usual Wilson lived by his own faith and standards. *His* courses were tough and so were his exams. At the end of his first year nearly a tenth of his students failed.

But Professor Wilson brought so much scholarship and brilliance into the classroom that he was able to have a tremendous effect on the young men. His command of language, his marvelous vocabulary, his years of training in expressing himself clearly, his sense of humor, his power of description gave them an inspiration they had not before experienced. He could make a scene in history live so that they never forgot it.

One of his students, Raymond B. Fosdick, wrote this about his lectures: "I still recall the vividness with which he described the scene in Greyfriars churchyard, when on a grim, forbidding Sunday morning in February, 1638, under the shadow of Edinburgh Castle, the stern and determined citizens of Scotland signed their names to the Covenant on a flat tombstone just outside the door. . . . To Wilson it was one of the outstanding events in the long struggle for liberty. It was here that freedom of conscience took its root . . ."

Another student has said that his lectures were really political addresses: "The students would frequently burst into spontaneous applause and cheer his remarks."

The thrill began when he walked into the room, and it lingered long after he had left. He was the public debater, the Gladstone, the member of Parliament, the responsible public officeholder in a free democratic society. The stimulation that he gave his students, of course, reacted upon himself as well, and he strove to give them more and more. And he belonged to his students after class was over, for private consultation, or on the athletic field cheering their games.

All of the triumphs and problems of his work were shared with Ellen and with his father. He still turned to his father as a teacher and depended upon his advice, and when at last Dr. Joseph Wilson consented to come and live with him at Princeton, Woodrow Wilson was completely happy about it. Ellen's brothers, Stockton and Edward, sometimes visited. Stockton Axson was an adult by this time, and Edward was studying to be a chemist. In the summer he worked at the Edison laboratories nearby and boarded in Princeton.

Their house at 72 Library Place was ample and lovely with carefully landscaped grounds. In fact, the town of Princeton had the kind of natural beauty that Wilson liked. It was very different from Staunton, Augusta, or Charlottesville, but its colonial houses and big-trunked trees that lined the streets did have something of the charming atmosphere of a Southern town. He thoroughly enjoyed spinning down its shady avenues on his bicycle.

The bicycle was an economy for which Wilson was grateful; and he was glad that he and other professors could use them. Because his salary was still not equal to his expenses, even though it was higher, he had as heavy a work schedule as usual, teaching, writing, lecturing at New York Law School and Johns Hopkins.

In the spring of 1893 bound copies of *Division and Reunion* appeared, and reviewers and readers alike discovered in it the depth of Wilson's tolerance and peace-loving compassion. Many Wilsonites, and even critics of Wilson, today believe that this was the finest piece of historical writing that he ever did.

In *Division and Reunion* he showed that as a Southerner he felt no bitterness, that he wanted any remaining divisions healed and the United States to be a whole and peaceable nation. He called the War with Mexico a "war of ruthless aggrandizement." In telling of the hundredth anniversary of the Declaration of Independence he said that "it was a fit symbol and assurance of the settled peace and prosperity which were in store for the country in the future. . . . It showed the economic resources of the South freed, like those of the North, for a rapid and unembarrassed development [at the end of Reconstruction]. . . . The stage was cleared for the creation of a new nation."

By the time that *Division and Reunion* appeared, Woodrow Wilson was completing his third year at Princeton and his eighth year of teaching college students, and he had arrived at some important conclusions about education in America. When he was invited to speak that summer at the Chicago World's Fair to the International Congress of Education, he set forth his views, and his audience found him astonishing.

He declared that the college had a responsibility to society and must train its students for a well-rounded life. Colleges in the United States were becoming too engrossed in specialization, he told his listeners. The college must give every student a liberal education first, before he takes up the study of a profession. A doctor must be able to face politics intelligently. A lawyer must understand his physical self and the universe.

He excited the learned gathering as he excited undergraduates.

"Our professional men are lamed and hampered by that partial knowledge which is the most dangerous form of ignorance. . . . Our faculties must make knowledge whole. . . . The empiric is the natural enemy of society and it is imperative that everything should be done—everything risked—to get rid of him. Nothing sobers and reforms him like a (genuine) liberal education."

At Princeton in the fall he continued to press for reforms in education at large and at Princeton in particular. His weight in faculty meetings was being felt more and more, and he and President Patton often locked horns.

When the students came to the faculty with a petition for the honor system, Woodrow Wilson promptly became their champion. He had faith in the integrity of young people, and if these students wanted to be put on their honor at exam time, for instance, instead of being policed like potential criminals, Professor Wilson believed they should have the opportunity to prove themselves honorable gentlemen. The faculty meeting that considered the petition was tense. President Patton ridiculed the idea. Professor Wilson argued with cool, calm dignity, and won the day.

The students would have died for him after that.

"Professor Wilson is fair!"

"He is absolutely fair!"

During this year and the next, Woodrow Wilson visited parts of the United States that he had not seen before: invitations to speak and lecture made this possible. Wherever he went he wrote Ellen every day about every detail; during the summer of 1894 he was sending her letters from Colorado.

"My first lecture has been so much talked about and has received so much praise that I am made the more nervous about the second one tonight." And a week later: "I am rejoiced to say that I not only keep my audience here, but draw new people at every lecture, till now I have quite a 'following.' "

Woodrow Wilson's following was growing slowly and surely all over the nation. His following of readers had already grown to the point where the New York publishing house of Harper & Brothers offered him a contract to write the huge work he had long ago dreamed about: a history of the American people in several volumes to compare with Green's *Short History of the English People.*

It would mean work, work, work, but he had learned to budget his time so carefully that he knew how to accomplish more than most men in a day.

No matter how much work he took on, he planned his hours so that there was always time for his family. Meals were the same joyous event they had been in his own childhood home. He read to his three little girls, and he and Ellen read aloud together, and the family circle now included Ellen's sister Margaret, who had come to live with them. Margaret had not yet reached her teens, and she adored her brother-in-law, even though he was a strict foster father at times, or seemed so to her.

Their house was rather crowded, Woodrow and Ellen admitted, and they were both tired of renting. Since they would obviously be in Princeton for many years, probably for the rest of their lives, why not build a house of their own?

They purchased a piece of land at 50 Library Place, full of old oak trees, a sycamore, and a glowing copper beech. The house was to be stone halfway up and white stucco trimmed with dark brown wood above, with sharp gables. The architect and contractors kept them waiting nearly a year, but at last they moved in. Rooms enough for everyone! On the ground floor at the back of the house, safe from disturbance, was the professor's study, with his bookcase, a portrait of Daniel Webster, and one of Gladstone that Ellen had painted. Since they had inherited antiques from both sides of their family, the furnishings were lovely.

Mrs. Bliss Perry, wife of one of the other professors, dropped by late in the day that they moved from one house to another, expecting to see packing boxes, rolled-up rugs, unhung pictures, and general confusion. She found everything in order and settled, and she stared at Mrs. Wilson in amazement.

Ellen Wilson just smiled and said, "I discovered long ago that it is as easy to hire fifteen helpers for one day as it is to hire one helper for fifteen days."

Professor Wilson himself was of no use when it came to household chores. The only task he could be trusted with was winding the grandfather clock on Saturday night.

His big responsibility was paying for the house. They had gone into considerable debt for it, and as usual everything had cost more than their estimates. There was nothing to do but take on extra lecturing tasks and work and overwork.

Woodrow Wilson had the same temperament and constitution that he had had as a younger man. He was still high strung and tense; his nervous and digestive systems still protested when they had had too much strain put upon them. Wilson was approaching forty; he had begun to feel an occasional twinge of arthritis here and there. During the spring of 1896 an attack of neuritis crippled his right hand into painful uselessness. He could not hold a pen in his hand, and he could not bear to touch the keys of the typewriter.

This sudden inability to work was horrifying when he thought of his commitments! He could dictate his letters to Ellen, and she could massage his afflicted hand and ease it with warm cloths. But the doctor advised a complete rest.

The gentle but firm Ellen Axson Wilson began making plans for that vacation abroad that she knew he had wanted for a long time. They *must* afford it whether they could or not, and she decided to manage it by staying at home herself.

Gradually the pain subsided and he recovered some of the use of his hand, but the trip to Europe was a determined fact, and Professor Wilson went aboard the *Ethiopia* bound for Glasgow on the thirtieth of May, his right hand resting in a silken sling. When the ship stood out to sea he breathed deeply and paced up and down, feeling the restful effect almost at once, and long before she docked in Glasgow he was the center of jovial conversations with the other passengers.

From Glasgow he crossed Scotland to Edinburgh, with its great castle rising on sheer rock, its rows of granite gray houses on a cluster of hills as steep as those of Staunton. His own forebears had come from these Scottish Lowlands and so had some of Gladstone's.

During June Wilson visited every significant site that he could: the cottage where Robert Burns was born, Wordsworth's home at Rydal Mount in the Lake District of northern England, then farther south to Oxford University, and finally to London.

"My arm suffers scarcely a twinge," he wrote in one of his many long letters to Ellen.

He went to Wales and toured through the rolling green hills of the Wye River Valley, then back to other parts of England.

When he finally returned to 50 Library Place he was well, rested, eager to resume his schedule of teaching, lecturing, writing, and telling jokes at the dinner table to rouse the happy laughter of his three little girls and sister-in-law.

He returned to a significant year in American politics, a Presidential election to which tempers had been heating for a long time. Woodrow Wilson sat quietly at his desk and reflected on the American history that had occurred during the years he had been teaching at Bryn Mawr, Wesleyan, and Princeton.

The very narrow margin by which the Republicans had elected Garfield and Arthur sixteen years ago had raised tremendous hopes among Democratic Party leaders and workers. Four years later they had elected Grover Cleveland, the first Democratic President since the Civil War. But Cleveland had had no talent for popularity, and he had antagonized many pressure groups. His veto of an overlarge veterans' pension bill had damaged him badly. Gradually the Democratic margin melted away. The Republicans who had given Cleveland their support reverted to their own party. When Cleveland ran for re-election, he won by a very narrow margin in the popular vote, but he lost in the Electoral College because Benjamin Harrison carried the big states of Indiana and New York.

During the campaign the Republicans had promised pensions to veterans and their dependents, and high tariffs; and these promises were enthusiastically kept. In 1890, the year that the Wilsons came to Princeton, the McKinley Tariff Act was passed, providing the highest protective tariff the United States had ever had, and low- or no-protective-tariff advocates like Woodrow Wilson were appalled that the men in Congress could not see the dangers in shutting out foreign goods and cutting off the United States from world trade. America could not possibly consume all the things she made herself. If she would not buy from other countries, she could not expect them to buy from her. This was a way to bring about a depression at home and create enemies abroad.

The wild spending of the "Billion Dollar Congress" of 1890, and the hot debates all over the country about the wisdom of the McKinley tariff, tipped the scales once more in the Presidential election of 1892, and Grover Cleveland went back into office, with Adlai E. Stevenson of Illinois as his Vice-President. The party won control of both Houses of Congress, too.

The Democratic Party came back into power just as the depression that so many had been predicting began to develop. It became the "Panic of 1893." Railroads went into receivership; banks closed; thousands were thrown out of work. There were hunger marches, riots, strikes in different parts of the country.

Political leaders debated fiercely as to what they thought the causes of the depression were. Another issue that received much attention was the national currency. The United States then was on the gold standard; that is, the official national currency was based on gold of a certain weight and fineness, and the value of all other forms of United States money was figured in terms of it. The government bought gold at a fixed price and made it into coins. This was called "free coinage" of gold, and the price of gold remained constant as a result.

Silver-mining interests resented this arrangement, and before the panic, during the heyday of the Billion Dollar Congress, they had forced passage of a bill requiring the government to buy a certain amount of silver each month and support its price. They forced its passage by threatening the defeat of the McKinley Tariff Act.

This was not the sort of conduct that Woodrow Wilson regarded as "responsible leadership," and reading such news had added to the tensions that brought on his neuritis. The four years of Cleveland's second term in office saw some corrective measures, such as the repeal of the Silver Purchase Act and partial recovery from the panic; but when Professor Wilson returned from his vacation in 1896 the national issues were essentially the same: high tariffs versus low; silver versus gold.

The Republican and Democratic National Conventions had been held while Wilson was abroad, and in each party by that time an extraordinary and melodramatic personality was developing.

In Republican ranks more and more was being heard from and about Theodore Roosevelt of New York. Teddy Roosevelt had been a member of the New York State Assembly at one time; then he had gone to a cattle ranch to bronco-bust his way back to health. After his return to New York he became one of the three commissioners of the United States Civil Service in Benjamin Harrison's administration, and by the time the Republican Convention met in St. Louis in June, 1896, he was president of the Board of Police Commissioners in New York City and an influential voice in his party.

The dramatic figure of the Democratic Convention, which was held in Chicago in July of that same year, was William Jennings Bryan of Nebraska. Bryan, the Great Commoner, was a broad-shouldered, bullnecked, and forceful fellow who swept audiences along with his emotional oratory. William Jennings Bryan was about three years younger than Wilson, born in Illinois and a graduate of the Union College of Law in Chicago. He had been living in Nebraska for nearly a decade, and it was in that state that he began to be prominent in politics. He was in Congress for two terms, then editor of the Omaha *World Herald,* and his gift for making exciting speeches made him a popular lecturer at Chautauquas. He pleaded for free coinage of silver at every opportunity. By the time of the Democratic Convention in 1896 he was the champion of the silver bloc. At that convention he made his famous "Cross of Gold" speech:

"If they dare to come out in the open field and defend the gold standard as a good thing we will fight them to the uttermost. Having behind us the producing masses of this nation and the world, supported by the commercial interests, the laboring interests, and the toilers everywhere, we will answer their demand for a gold standard by saying to them: You shall not press down upon the brow of labor this crown of thorns. You shall not crucify mankind upon a cross of gold."

The convention went wild with joy and nominated him for the Presidency. He had united them; he had given them their battle cry: silver, silver, silver!

Returning from Europe a few weeks after, Wilson read Bryan's speech with great care and considerable disgust. Here was certainly careless leadership in his own party, and it worried him deeply.

But the worry about Bryan's oratory had to wait for a more immediate and pressing assignment. In October the College of New Jersey was celebrating its sesquicentennial, and Woodrow Wilson had been invited to make a key address. At these ceremonies the College of New Jersey was to become Princeton University, and Woodrow Wilson chose the subject, "Princeton in the Nation's Service."

Professor Wilson felt the weight of his task very deeply. He knew what views he intended to express, but his speech lacked a forceful opening sentence. He worried about it for days on end, until at last one day it came to him:

"Princeton pauses to look back upon her past, not as an old man grown reminiscent, but as a prudent man still in his youth and lusty prime and at the threshold of new tasks, who would remind himself of his origin and lineage, recall the pledges of his youth, and assess as at a turning in his life the duties of his station."

He looked happily at the words he had typed out, and

sat back in his chair with a sense of deep satisfaction.

Peddling down Nassau Street on his bicycle later in the day, he rode hard to catch up with the horse-drawn carriage of a fellow teacher, and shouted up to him, "I've decided on my opening sentence. That means the battle is won."

All of Princeton was excited about the sesquicentennial. It was a great milestone for the historic village and the college-turned-university. After Dr. Wilson's speech they would realize that it was to be a milestone in American education as well. The buildings along Nassau Street were gay with bunting and orange pennants, and a huge archway had been built over the street with the words, "From the Town to the University." President and Mrs. Cleveland had accepted an invitation to appear, so had Mark Twain, Booker T. Washington, J. P. Morgan, and a star-studded list of other celebrities would be present at some point in the three days of festivities.

On the first morning, October 20, 1896, an impressive and solemn parade passed under the arch led by President Patton, the trustees, faculty, and representatives from other colleges. In the afternoon they heard an address by President Charles W. Eliot of Harvard, and in the evening Walter Damrosch conducted a concert.

The town was crowded with visitors, many of them were alumni from every class, and the news that Professor Wilson '79 was the principal speaker on the second day drew a large delegation of Seventy-niners. They sat together in packed Alexander Hall to look proudly at Tommy Wilson on the rostrum as he was introduced by one of the trustees of the new university.

From the moment that Professor Wilson began to speak, his audience was with him, and its enthusiasm mounted as the drama and forthright tones of his message developed and ascended. He reviewed the history of the college that had been "founded upon the very eve of the stirring changes which put this drama [American Revolution] on the stage." He reminded them that James Madison and "Light Horse" Harry Lee had been among their graduates, that nine Princeton men sat in the Constitutional Convention of 1787. When he said that "Princeton has formed practical men, whom the world could trust to do its daily work like men of honor," the younger faculty members, who had been sharing his struggle with President Patton, knew he was going right to the heart of the matter.

"It used to be taken for granted," Mr. Wilson went on, "that colleges would be found always on the conservative side in politics (except on the question of free trade); but in this latter day a great deal has taken place which goes far toward discrediting the presumption. The college in our day lies very near indeed to the affairs of the world. It is a place of the latest experiments; its laboratories are brisk with the spirit of discovery. . . . There is no radical like a learned radical, bred in the schools; and thoughts of revolution have in our time been harbored in universities . . ."

The firm-chinned quiet courage of the speaker made

spines tingle. Several times his audience interrupted him with applause.

He called himself "a student of society" with no "laboratory but the world of books and men," and he warned his audience that science could bring them physical comforts and progress, and with its help men were breaking with the past and coming into a new world. But they must not forget what they could learn from the past. They must keep faith with the past as a preparation for leadership in days of social change. . . . "There is laid upon us the compulsion of the national life. We dare not keep aloof and closet ourselves while a nation comes to its maturity. The days of glad expansion are gone, our life grows tense and difficult; our resource for the future lies in careful thought, providence, and a wise economy; and the school must be of the nation.

"I have had sight of the perfect place of learning in my thought; a free place, and a various, where no man could be and not know with how great a destiny knowledge had come into the world . . . the home of sagacious men, hardheaded and with a will to know, debaters of the world's questions every day and used to the rough ways of democracy . . . a place where ideals are kept in heart in an air they can breathe; but no fool's paradise. A place where to hear the truth about the past and hold debate about the affairs of the present, with knowledge and without passion. . . . Who shall show us the way to this place?"

The Seventy-niners rose to their feet, cheering! The whole audience broke into applause.

Mrs. Wilson's eyes were brimming when she left the hall upon his arm, and she almost lost him in the crowd that pressed about him to clasp his hand.

She wrote to a friend the next day, "The grandest thing of the sort, everyone says, that America has ever seen. It was the most brilliant—dazzling—success from first to last. And such an ovation as Woodrow received! I never imagined anything like it. And think of so delighting such an audience, the most distinguished, everyone says, that has ever been assembled in America; —famous men from all parts of Europe . . . As for the Princeton men some of them simply fell on his neck and wept for joy."

8. Campus Warfare

INVITATIONS to Professor Wilson to speak at other colleges and universities increased, and as he traveled around the United States on his lecturing assignments he kept in close touch with national and world affairs. McKinley defeated Bryan at the polls in November, 1896.

The major incident of the first McKinley administration was a tragedy: the Spanish-American War. "We want no wars of conquest. We must avoid the temptation of territorial aggression," McKinley had said in his inaugural address, but there were others in his administration who felt otherwise, and McKinley did not have sufficient strength for his own convictions. Theodore Roosevelt, now Assistant Secretary of the Navy, and Senator Henry Cabot Lodge of Massachusetts were among the Republican Party leaders demanding that the United States be firm in demanding independence for Cuba. Cuba had been in revolt against Spanish rule for years, they argued. They also wanted to see Spain out of the Caribbean. And they wanted the United States to become a "world power," imperialistic, a militant influence in world affairs. While they made rousing speeches, careless newspapers —the yellow press—aroused public sentiment with melodramatic reports of lurid conditions and atrocities in Cuba.

Woodrow Wilson wanted to see America go on growing as she was, but he did not want her to be careless with her strength. Many thoughtful people felt that way, but in January, 1898, riots broke out in Havana, and the U. S. battleship, the *Maine,* was sent to Cuba to protect United States citizens living there. While she lay at anchor in Havana harbor, she was blown up by persons unknown and 260 of her officers and men were killed.

The news blazed in the papers, and public sentiment already hot became hotter. The United States government delivered an ultimatum to the Spanish government, demanding peace and self-government in Cuba.

President McKinley received word that Spain agreed to the terms of the ultimatum, but the warmongers were crying, "Remember the *Maine!*" President McKinley, not at all a strong leader, nor a very responsible one by Wilson's standards, listened to his saber-rattling advisers and went before Congress with a war message anyway. In April Congress adopted a resolution recognizing Cuban independence, and two days later war was declared between Spain and the United States.

Once declared, the war was not limited to the Caribbean, because Spain also owned the Philippine Islands in the far Pacific. The Philippines were conquered by part of the United States Navy in the battle of Manila Bay, and the battle of San Juan Hill brought the war to an end in Cuba in July. It was in this engagement that Theodore Roosevelt, as commander of his Rough Riders, became such a popular national hero and political figure.

Meanwhile, Czar Nicholas II of Russia was calling a disarmament conference at The Hague for the summer of 1899, and when at last it convened, twenty-six nations were represented. After the deep embarrassment that many in the United States felt about America's flamboyant behavior toward Spain, it was deeply comforting to realize that the delegation from the United States to the first Hague Peace Conference had been influential in creating a Permanent Court of International Arbitration.

Wilson was able to be in Europe himself that summer with Stockton Axson on a much needed holiday that a group of Princeton men had made possible. Many alumni had been worrying about the amount of energy he had to expend on lecture trips in order to earn enough income for his family. They wanted him to give his whole self to the university. Eight of them, including the generous Cleveland H. Dodge and Cyrus H. McCormick, drew up an agreement to add $2400 a year to his salary for five years, so that he could give up his outside lecturing, devote himself to Princeton teaching, and replenish himself in the summer with restful travel. He himself had asked the question, "Who shall show us the way?" and they were convinced that he was the person to give Princeton the leadership it needed.

The schism between old guard and new blood on the campus was deepening, and into the breach were drawn all sorts of public questions. One of these was evolution, Darwin's theory that all plant and animal forms are constantly changing and evolving new forms. President Patton was opposed to evolution. Wilson felt that every new idea deserved an open-minded inquiry. In those days the theories of socialism and communism were beginning to make a serious stir. Wilson said, "Gentlemen, let us study them and discover to our own satisfaction or disappointment what they are all about."

Wilson was no radical. He knew that a student who delved into a theory of government and found it lacking could never be persuaded to it by speechmakers. This was what he meant by a college's responsibility to the nation: preparing its students for life in a democratic society with a sound, all-round education.

There were so many reforms needed at Princeton! But with President Patton at the helm reform was practically impossible, and Woodrow Wilson began to wonder whether he was not beating his head against a stone wall. Perhaps he ought to ask for a year's leave to study abroad. Or, why not resign altogether and devote himself to writing? His *Division and Reunion* and *The State* were both still selling, and his *History of the American People* was nearing completion.

Free-lance writing, he reflected, would give him more time at home with his family. His daughters were growing so fast that they seemed changed to him when he had been away only a few weeks. He wanted to enjoy every minute of their growing-up.

Margaret was thirteen, Jessie was twelve, and Eleanor ten. His sister-in-law, Margaret Axson, was now old enough to receive young men callers. His brother-in-law Stockton Axson, even dearer to him than Heath Dabney, had come to live with the family, because he had joined the Princeton faculty. Edward was with them too, and so was Woodrow's father. They made a big circle around the dinner table.

If he were free-lancing, he could give more time to his church, too. He and Ellen had finally joined the second of the two Presbyterian churches, and he had never given up the hope of bringing together the two congregations.

Thoughts of home and freedom filled his mind as the family planned their Christmas and New Year's festivities. The three daughters prepared the house with lovely hangings and decorations, and everyone hung his stocking along the second-floor railing, because the fireplace wasn't big enough to hold them all. On Christmas Eve they sang carols, and again on Christmas morning, and after breakfast they exchanged presents.

Woodrow and Ellen usually exchanged a wink and ate as slowly as possible, while the younger generation sat bursting with impatience.

Christmas and New Year's were the times, in particular, when everyone counted on Woodrow Wilson for happy nonsense, for jigs and limericks and stories, in Scottish and Irish brogue. And they counted on him to lead them in old ballads.

"Good Lord deliver us from witches and warlocks and from things that say woo-oo in the night," he always intoned on New Year's Eve.

At midnight they sang "Auld Lang Syne" and then rushed to fling open the front door to let the old year out and the new year in.

Oh, there could be more, much more, of this rich family living if he were to resign his professorship!

Others on the faculty and board were just as discouraged as he, and at last one of the trustees wrote Dr. Patton a sharp letter and urged him to resign.

Dr. Patton was shrewd enough to outfox his enemies with one final gesture. He not only resigned; he recommended Woodrow Wilson to take his place as president. He did it, because he knew that many of the trustees had that exact idea in mind.

With great gusto the trustees accepted Dr. Patton's advice, and Woodrow Wilson was unanimously elected the next president of Princeton University.

President of Princeton! A chance to put into effect his ideas about higher education. Thoughts of free-lancing were swept aside as students rushed to his house and carried him off to the steps of Nassau Hall.

"A speech! A speech!" they shouted happily, and in a voice hoarse and a little choked he complied.

Woodrow and Ellen had to leave the house they loved so much (eventually they sold it) and move into "Prospect," the president's official residence on the campus. There they did more formal entertaining than they had ever done in their lives before. Prospect had a huge drawing room for receptions and teas and a huge dining room for dinner parties.

President Wilson's inauguration ceremony in October, 1902, was as gay as the sesquicentennial with banners, bunting, parades, prominent persons, and speeches. Woodrow Wilson shared his dreams for Princeton with his audience. He foresaw a vigorous and effective university. Princeton was going to produce informed and thoughtful men, and they would be sent into the world not "to sit still and know" but to act. Princeton could supply America with "men who care more for principles than for money."

None was happier than his aged father. Grateful that he had been permitted to live long enough to see this triumph, Dr. Joseph Wilson, now propped up on pillows in bed, addressed his three granddaughters who stood at his bed.

"Never forget what I tell you. Your father is the greatest man I have ever known."

"Oh, we know that, Grandfather," said Margaret.

"I've lived a long time, Margaret," he rebuked her, "and I know what I'm talking about. This is just the beginning of a very great career."

From Heath Dabney came the message, "Who could have guessed that an Illimitable Idiot would ever be selected the president of a great university?"

Woodrow Wilson took up his tasks as president on a flood tide of good will and cooperation. The trustees voted him extraordinary authority to go ahead, and when he reported to them that he would need an additional six million dollars for increased faculty, more buildings, a system of preceptors, they agreed, and he worked with them to raise the money. He wrote to wealthy men who could donate if they would; he spoke to Princeton alumni groups and told them point blank that if they wanted the kind of university they claimed they wanted they would have to dig into their pockets for it.

His first four years as president of Princeton made a glorious success story, during which Princeton became the rival of the finest universities in the country. He overhauled the entire curriculum, stiffened entrance exams, and raised the scholastic requirements in every course. Lazy young men began to disappear from the campus, and during his first year as president a quarter of the students flunked out. The whole university became pervaded with an atmosphere of real scholarship, genuine thinking, and the joy of searching for and discovering what Woodrow Wilson called "the spirit of learning."

His biggest idea during those four years was his system of preceptors, very similar to a system used at Oxford University in England. He had explained the plan in his inaugural address: "The new preceptors will take some part in the lecture and regular class work . . . they will be members of the faculty, indistinguishable in privilege and rank from their colleagues." In fact, these fifty young men, whom he engaged from all over the United States, had a rank equivalent to assistant professor. They were all brilliant and promising scholars in their fields, and many of them eventually became full professors. Thus, instead of a few overworked teachers, there was an instructor for every five or six undergraduates. To have a preceptor meant to have personal guidance and attention, to have small group discussions, to have individual help with assignments.

Other universities watched Princeton's experiment, and it proved so successful that they soon adopted it. The plan is still a vital part of university life in America. The preceptor plan has changed with the changing times as all good systems should, but Woodrow Wilson's original experiment started it.

He himself developed one secret complaint about the system. Too many of the Princeton preceptors were attractive young bachelors, and too many of them were calling on his daughters.

There were a few shadows in the private life of the

Wilsons during those four years of success. Dr. Joseph Wilson had been failing steadily, and the most heart-breaking part of his illness was to see his mind fail and to watch him return to the helplessness of a child. Woodrow Wilson sat by his bedside, talking to him when he could understand, singing his favorite hymns. At last during January of Wilson's first year as president, Dr. Joseph Wilson died.

The next family tragedy was Ellen's. Her younger brother, Edward, by now married with a small child, was drowned with his family in a ferry boat accident.

Because they were people of staunch faith, Ellen and Woodrow Wilson came through each trial with quiet dignity, concentrating on tasks and responsibilities for comfort and discipline. In the summer of 1903 they were able to take a restful trip to Europe together.

In the fall of 1904 Theodore Roosevelt ran for re-election against Judge Alton B. Parker of New York State. Roosevelt, who had been Vice-President with McKinley during his second term, had stepped into the Presidency upon the death of McKinley. Republican Roosevelt's popularity as a hero of the Spanish-American War won the day. He was a swashbuckling extrovert, a rousing campaigner; the public was becoming reform-minded, and so was he. He denounced big business mergers that made free competition impossible and forced out small businessmen. He encouraged anti-trust legislation and traveled around the country making trust-busting speeches against the oil interests, the railroad holding companies, the steel combines. Of course, it was easier to denounce them than to change them, but he built his campaign upon denouncing them and won.

William Jennings Bryan, now editor and founder of a weekly paper called *The Commoner,* was the leader of the Democratic Party, somewhat to Wilson's regret. Wilson was a conservative himself where national finances were concerned, and he felt that Bryan's "free silver" ideas would be bad for the economy.

Wilson was himself a national figure by then with tremendous popularity among people who attended his lectures all over the country, and his own persisting interest in national politics convinced many that he could be as effective in public office as he was at the head of a university.

The Lotos Club, whose membership was made up entirely of prominent men, gave one of its "State Dinners" in his honor in New York City in February, 1906. George Harvey, who had succeeded Walter Page as head of Harper & Brothers, gave the speech introducing Woodrow Wilson.

"It is with a sense almost of rapture that I contemplate even the remotest possibility of casting a ballot for the president of Princeton University to become President of the United States," he said.

"Was Mr. Harvey joking?" asked Ellen in surprise the next day.

"He didn't seem to be joking," her husband replied.

After the Lotos Club dinner Wilson's friends fell into the habit of referring to him as Presidential timber.

State officeholding was considered a logical step toward such a nomination. In New Jersey he had already been discussed as a possible candidate for the legislature, and he was a member of the New Jersey Commission on Uniform State Laws. Perhaps the role of responsible officeholder would come to him some day after all; it was not too late, really; he was only fifty. His mind was certainly as clear and creative as ever.

In fact, being in a position at last to put his most progressive ideas into effect stimulated him to have more ideas, each bigger than the last. He was exhilarated by the flowering of his university. Princeton would be for the nation's service in every sense. She would be America's most splendid example of true democratic life.

"We cannot stop here," he told his associates.

He was drawing up a plan to reorganize the undergraduate social life and bring an end to campus snobbery and group separateness.

He presented his newest plan to the trustees at their meeting in December, 1906. It was inspired, he told them, by the same English universities that had inspired his preceptorial system. There were on the campus social differences between upper and lower classmen, between club members and those who were not elected to any club. He wanted to see the campus divided into residential quadrangles or colleges, and in each members of all four classes would be assigned to live so that they could mingle socially, eat together, study together, live together on a basis of equality. When a man goes out to live in a free democratic society he must mingle with—and get along with—all kinds. Then let his college train him for this. Such clubs as "Ivy," "Cap and Gown," and "Tiger Inn" grew more snobbish with each passing year, and this influence was bad for the young men.

The first reaction of the trustees to the "Quad Plan" was favorable; all but one gave it tentative approval. But as the idea spread over the faculty and alumni grapevine, the opposition began to rise. It rose to the proportions of a cyclone.

Andrew F. West, Dean of the Graduate School, quickly became the leader of the opposition. He had rather fancied himself as president of the university, and so had his friends, when the post went to Wilson. This could be a chance to retaliate.

The chief argument against the Quad Plan was that it would be extremely expensive, which it certainly would, and the Westites wanted the money spent on building a separate graduate school. While Wilson favored a graduate school, his Quad Plan seemed more important to him. He debated the issue through several faculty and board meetings, standing his ground, absolute, uncompromising.

Opposition grew steadily stronger until the Board of

Trustees reversed itself, and at its meeting on October 17, 1907, voted that "the President be requested to withdraw the plan."

Shocked and stunned, Wilson went stiffly out of the meeting room. He had been given an overwhelming vote of no confidence by his board, and out of the depths of his hurt he wondered whether he ought to resign. This was his first real defeat, and it proved a bitter experience. But as he strode across the campus he determined not to give up the idea of his Quad Plan. There would be another time, another year to present it again.

Within the shelter of the happy household that he and Ellen had created together there was healing comfort—in the warm company of his beautiful young daughters, in the quiet meditation in his book-lined study. He had been living too tensely; his neuritis was at times extremely painful; and only last summer he had experienced a burst blood vessel in his left eye. At that time the physician had told him that he was beginning to have hardening of the arteries and advised him to retire.

But "retire" was a word that Woodrow Wilson never understood. He had his responsibilities, no matter how many wounds they must require him to sustain, responsibilities to his students, his publishers, his country. He must follow national affairs carefully. William Jennings Bryan's speeches seemed to be growing more careless every day.

"If only we could do something at once dignified and effective, to knock Mr. Byran once and for all into a cocked hat!" Wilson had recently written to a friend.

Bryan's motive became steadily clearer as the summer of 1908 approached, and he was once more nominated to be the Democratic candidate for the Presidency. The Republicans nominated William Howard Taft, a conservative lawyer from Ohio, head of the Philippine Commission under McKinley, and President Theodore Roosevelt's Secretary of War.

About the same time the problem of the graduate school at Princeton appeared to be solved when the trustees voted to accept a bequest for a graduate school to be built on the campus. Wilson's heartache was eased by the action, even though he would rather have had the money for his Quad Plan. With the graduate school built, his Quad Plan could be next.

But his defeat over the Quad Plan had shocked him very deeply. By summertime he had reached his limit in nervous exhaustion, and he sailed for Europe and the brisk, invigorating air of the Lake District and the Scottish lowlands, even before the Democratic Convention had completed its slate. When he heard rumors that he might be considered as the Vice-Presidential nominee, he said to Stockton Axson before he left:

"If they approach you on this, you are to decline it."

When he returned in September it was to learn that his friend Cleveland H. Dodge was trying to persuade Andrew Carnegie to donate the money to build the

Quads, and to see Taft elected to the Presidency in a strong Republican year. Taft had run against not only the regular Democratic candidate but Populist, Socialist, Prohibition Party, Socialist Labor, and Independence Party candidates.

Woodrow Wilson also returned to his greatest crisis as president of Princeton University. Dean West wanted the graduate school located off the campus where it would be less under President Wilson's jurisdiction. But the bequest had specified that it must be on the campus and so the majority stood with Wilson on this point—for a while.

Dean West was a shrewd man, and his campaign to get the graduate school away from the campus went on all winter. To help him, a wealthy graduate, William Cooper Procter, a soap manufacturer in Cincinnati, offered Princeton half a million dollars if the university could match it with another half million for a graduate school to be located on certain property considerably removed from the campus.

The university and its president were plunged into fierce politics by that offer. All spring and into the next fall Wilson spoke and argued and pleaded with faculty, trustees, and alumni not to allow the pressure of wealth to influence their thinking. The democratic intent of the Quad Plan had been lost under the same kind of pressure—the privilege of money—and he could not let them do this again. If West were able to draw away the graduate school, leaving Wilson in effect only president of the undergraduate portion, the creative body of the university would be cut in two.

The administration was already divided into Wilson supporters and West supporters.

"A danger surrounding our modern education is the danger of wealth," Wilson said to one meeting. "So far as the colleges go, the side-shows have swallowed up the circus, and we don't know what is going on in the main tent: and I don't know that I want to continue as ringmaster under those conditions."

As he wrote and spoke for his university he was attracting more and more public attention to his own ability, and in the May issue of *Harper's Weekly* George Harvey repeated his prophecy:

"We now expect to see Woodrow Wilson elected Governor of the State of New Jersey in 1910 and nominated for the Presidency in 1912 upon a platform demanding tariff revision downward."

1910 was only a few months away!

Editor Harvey had mentioned tariff because it was one of the hottest national issues of the day, and it was splitting the Republican Party in two. Senator Robert M. La Follette of Wisconsin and others were opposed to high tariffs and were fighting the Taft group on it, and so was Theodore Roosevelt.

Soon the *North American Review* asked Woodrow Wilson to write an article on the subject, and it appeared in the October, 1909, issue: "Tariff Make-Believe."

The next month another article by Wilson appeared in *Scribner's Magazine,* called "What Is a College For?"

"The college is for the use of the nation, not for the satisfaction of those who administer it or for the carrying out of their private views," he wrote. "It is for the training of men who are to rise above the ranks."

And what was happening to Princeton! It was being usurped by privilege. More and more the trustees were inclined to accept the Procter offer of half a million.

"I cannot accede to the acceptance of gifts upon terms which take the educational policy of the university out of the hands of the trustees and the faculty and permit it to be determined by those who give money," declared Wilson.

This was to be a real showdown between West and Wilson, and by the middle of January Wilson's influence was proved the stronger. The trustees rejected the Procter offer.

Interest in the controversy had become nationwide, and *The New York Times* asked Woodrow Wilson for advice in writing an informative editorial on it. He sat down at his typewriter immediately and wrote the *Times* a long careful explanation of his views. On February 3, 1910, the editorial appeared, denouncing "special privilege" and showing Woodrow Wilson to be the champion of the true democratic life.

The West faction was furious about the way Wilson had outfoxed them by giving the story to the *Times* himself, and many felt that he had been hasty.

It appeared, though, that the graduate-school controversy was finished—in triumph for Wilson.

Not so.

Dean West, just like Wilson, enjoyed friendships that dated way back into his youth. One of them was with a man named Isaac C. Wyman who lived in Salem, Massachusetts. About three months after the *Times* editorial, Mr. Wyman died and in his will he left Princeton two million dollars for a graduate college and made Dean West a co-trustee of the money.

When Woodrow Wilson received the news in a telegram, he laughed bitterly and said to Ellen, "We have beaten the living, but we cannot fight the dead. The game is up."

It was President Wilson's second great defeat.

Now he must decide whether or not to resign from his post. While the question boiled in his mind, he disciplined himself to reserved dignity as he proceeded with plans for the June commencement. This was the kind of time in which Woodrow Wilson seemed coldest and most unapproachable, when he was demanding the utmost of himself in proper deportment. The undergraduates expected the best of their president, and he was still their president. Dean West was a staff member and so were many of West's supporters. But they must work together for this last function of the year.

Every student on the campus knew the story of the West-Wilson feud, and at graduation time the senior class gave their president such a terrific ovation that his reserve melted away and he cried. Their president was a man of such conviction, such single-mindedness, that he could not change his course no matter what the price to himself. They became alumni with his baccalaureate sermon ringing in their memories:

"Princeton does not consist, has never consisted, of you and your classmates. Here men come and go, the men of her faculty and trustees as well as the men of her classes, but her force is not abated. She fails not of the impressions she makes. Her men are formed from generation to generation as if by a spirit that survives all persons and all circumstances. . . ."

9. Governor of New Jersey

LOYAL friends begged Wilson not to resign as president of the university. The anti-Wilson group saw an opportunity to force his resignation.

He was too sick at heart to make an immediate decision about it or about the committee from the Democratic Party that was trying to obtain an audience with him. He knew what they wanted. Ever since the beginning of the year George Harvey had been trying to persuade Wilson to run for governor.

"I don't want to see them," he said to Ellen.

He and Ellen were planning to spend a restful few weeks in Lyme, Connecticut, and they went ahead with their plans.

His session with campus politics had been quite enough for a while; he was tired, deeply tired. What could running for the governorship gain him except to have his name connected with the corruptions of machine politics? After twenty years of living in New

Jersey, he was familiar enough with the state's political situation.

New Jersey was known as the "home of the trusts," because her laws favored holding companies and gave special tax exemptions to corporations. The biggest trusts in the United States at the time were New Jersey corporations, and big property-owning interests like railroads and utilities enjoyed so many tax exemptions that other property owners had to make up the difference. Industrial interests made big donations to the political party machine that favored them, and for the last several years this had been the machine of the Republican Party.

Woodrow Wilson knew that there were many responsible leaders in both parties who wanted the conditions in the state changed, and they, like himself, wanted election laws reformed and gambling and betting outlawed. The spirit of reform that men like Theodore Roosevelt, William Jennings Bryan, and Robert La Follette had been making popular all over the country was just as popular in New Jersey.

In the Democratic Party in New Jersey, James Smith, Jr., a former United States Senator, from Newark, and Robert Davis in Jersey City were the progressive Democratic leaders who wanted reform. In the Republican Party George L. Record, in particular, was fighting his own party's machine in Hudson County. The situation was ready for a change if a dynamic candidate could be found to run for governor on the Democratic ticket, and Smith, Davis, George Harvey of *Harper's,* and others were making it quite clear to Woodrow Wilson that they considered him that man.

Burdened by the need to make two major decisions that would affect the lives of every member of his family—to remain at Princeton or to resign, to go into politics or to remain out—Woodrow Wilson, Ellen, and their three daughters settled down in rooms at "Miss Florence's" in Lyme for a secluded holiday.

After he had rested his mind would be clear enough to make a sound decision. He played golf in the warm summer air, and Ellen sat before her easel, painting.

"This is the hardest decision of Father's life," said his daughter Eleanor.

After they had gone to bed the girls could hear their parents talking in low tones late into the night, searching for wisdom.

One evening as the family sat around after dinner the telephone shattered their peace. Dr. Wilson answered it, and when he was through talking he said to Ellen: "It was Colonel Harvey. They have asked me to go to Deal Beach on Sunday for a conference with Watterson and Smith."

Tension seized everyone. Henry Watterson, they knew, was editor of the powerful *Louisville Courier-Journal.* But with profound relief Wilson's family heard him send a wire to Colonel Harvey, saying that there was no train from Lyme on Sunday. He could not attend the conference.

It seemed over, and the Wilsons chattered with happy relief. Sunday morning came, and all five of them were about to set out for church. Suddenly a stranger appeared at the door.

"Colonel Harvey has asked me to drop in and bring you down to dinner this evening," he explained. Then he added, "I'm instructed to bring you back or commit hara-kiri."

Ellen turned back into the house to pack Woodrow's bag, and in another few minutes he had kissed them all good-by and set off in a taxi for New London, where he and his escort caught a southbound train.

Eagerly the men clasped his hand one after another as he entered the house at Deal Beach, and earnestly they sat down to sober-faced planning. Wilson made it clear at once to Smith, head of the Newark and Essex County machine, which really controlled the New Jersey Democratic Party, that he would promise no favors to any machine. If he were elected, his would be "responsible leadership."

This was Colonel Watterson's first exposure to Wilson's personality, and as he listened to the conversation between Smith and Wilson, he caught fire.

"Dr. Wilson," he said enthusiastically, "if you are elected Governor of New Jersey in November, I'll take off my coat for you in 1912!"

It was done! Woodrow Wilson was their man!

The decision freed Wilson of his tensions, and it even eased the hurt he still felt from his two Princeton defeats. He liked a contest, whether it was on a debating platform, on the football field, or in an election. Exhilaration brewed inside him all the way back to Connecticut, and when he walked into the room where his family of women was waiting, his eyes sparkled with his old sense of humor.

"Tell us what happened!"

"What did you decide to do?"

They all clamored at once for news.

"Wait a minute," he said, "I want to show you what I found."

He took a new type of golf tee out of his pocket, set it on the floor with a golf ball on it, and proceeded to explain its advantages to them. When they had nearly burst with exasperation, he laughed happily and said:

"I have accepted the nomination, and I am absolutely free of pledges."

"Then you are the next governor, Father!"

"And the next President!"

"Not yet," he cautioned. "I must first be nominated, and then I must be elected."

Nominations in New Jersey were by party convention, and in the September primaries the delegates to the convention were elected. There was considerable opposition to Wilson's nomination by party men who wanted someone they could "handle," but with the support of men like Smith in Essex, together with the fine impression Wilson always made upon audiences, he rolled up a big plurality.

Nothing so exciting had happened in New Jersey politics for years, and the delegates gathered in the Taylor Opera House in Trenton in pandemonium. The hall and the streets outside were jammed. Princeton undergraduates had sent a cheering section. Progressives versus regulars! Pledged delegates versus free! Wild struggling of partisans through the crowded corridors to see this one, argue with that one, influence another vote! The meeting could scarcely contain itself through the nominating and seconding speeches.

It was Woodrow Wilson on the first ballot: 747½ votes out of a total of 1400 odd. Orators immediately began to shout that he would be the next President of the United States.

Wilson had been waiting at a nearby hotel, and when he was told the good news, he replied in a voice calm with discipline, which many mistook for coldness, "Thanks; I am ready."

He was rushed to the Opera House, where many were seeing him for the first time.

"Look at that jaw!" shouted one.

When the cheering at last subsided, he began his acceptance speech.

He was free of all pledges, he reminded them once more. "I did not seek this nomination. It has come to me absolutely unsolicited." There was to be no playing politics. "We are witnessing a renaissance of public spirit, a reawakening of sober public opinion, a revival of the power of the people."

Like young Princeton men, the Democratic Party

men were swept into his camp, and they were ready to go out and campaign in every corner of the state for him.

"A leader has come at last!"

One of the most important converts that Wilson made at that nominating convention was Joseph P. Tumulty, a powerful Hudson County Democrat, who had worked as hard as anyone to prevent Wilson's nomination. Now with complete abandon he hugged whoever was near him and joined in the shout:

"A leader! A leader at last!"

"The G.O.P. is in the soup!" said a gay letter from Heath Dabney.

Woodrow Wilson returned to Princeton in a tide of excitement, his melancholy cured. Now that he was a candidate for governor he *must* resign as president of Princeton. And there was a humorous side to it: if elected, he would automatically be, according to Princeton's regulations, her ex-officio president.

His first campaign speech was to be in Jersey City, in the densely populated railroad terminus controlled by the railroad interests. He did not want his wife or daughters to be present for this. If this first speech did not go well, he did not want them to witness his embarrassment.

But it wasn't just that first speech that he minded their attending, they soon discovered. He tried to keep them away from all of his speeches, and they quietly made their own plans for the campaign. Whenever

Margaret, Jessie, or Eleanor wanted to hear him, they would slip secretly into the back of the hall after it had filled up, so that their presence would not make him uneasy.

There was no need for him to feel uneasy, not after his appearance in Jersey City. Instead of the usual flowery, meaningless campaign oratory, he stepped forward to the edge of the platform to get as close as possible to his audience.

"If elected, as I expect to be," he told them, "I am left absolutely free to serve you with all singleness of purpose. It is a new era when these things can be said."

By Wilson standards it wasn't an outstanding speech, but the audience rose and cheered him at the end. From speech to speech, city to city, great crushes of people cheered him, because they trusted him, and they loved him for his straightforwardness and his sense of humor. The hour was never too tense for a joke, a funny story, or a limerick.

And he could take a kidding himself.

When a man in the audience shouted up to him, "Go it, Woody. You are all right. But you ain't no beaut," Wilson grinned and shouted back:

> "For beauty I am not a star;
> There are others handsomer, far;
> But my face, I don't mind it,
> For I am behind it;
> 'Tis the people in front that I jar."

All over the United States people were watching the results in New Jersey, because it was no secret that Wilson was considered Presidential timber. If he could succeed in overthrowing the old regime in New Jersey, if he could reform conditions there, then he would be one of the leading candidates at the national convention in 1912. The Wilson tide rolled up steadily until Election Day, and there was no doubt in anyone's mind about the results.

The Wilson family at Prospect sat about and walked about, unable to concentrate on any activity. New Jersey had not adopted woman suffrage, and Mrs. Wilson and her three daughters, all over twenty-one, could not vote. Of course, he was going to be elected, they told one another. He was going to be governor, and then he was going to be President.

The candidate was maddeningly calm, or pretended to be.

The telephone became the center of their lives when the polls closed, and it rang frequently. Every time Dr. Wilson answered it he would merely nod and say, "Most encouraging!"

By ten o'clock that night the election was secure. He had rolled up a plurality bigger even than the most optimistic prophecies, and the Democratic Party had captured both houses of the legislature.

Once more the Princeton campus and the grounds of Prospect were alive with cheering, happy mobs of students.

"A speech! A speech!" they shouted to him.

But this time Ellen would not allow it. He was too tired after his long, hard campaign. With her finest Southern graciousness she received many in the house —for a while—and at last when their excitement was spent, at least in part, she persuaded them all to go home.

She and Woodrow must plan to leave Prospect, but since New Jersey did not have a governor's mansion, they decided to put their furniture in storage and take three bedrooms and a drawing room at the Princeton Inn. It was a terribly public way to live, but Ellen, Margaret, Jessie, and Eleanor *knew* it would be unwise to buy a house in Trenton. They *knew* they would be moving again in two years. Since Margaret was studying singing and living in New York most of the time, Jessie was doing social work at the Lighthouse in Philadelphia, and Eleanor was commuting to Philadelphia daily to study art, they would be crowded only once in a while.

There was one redeeming factor. The state did furnish the governor with a summer house at Sea Girt, and during the summers the whole family could be together there and spread themselves out a bit.

But long before Governor Wilson could even think of enjoying a summer at the seashore—immediately after Election Day, in fact—he was heavily involved in a show-down fight with the politicians in his own party.

James Smith, Jr., Democratic boss in Essex County,

had thrown his resources into electing Wilson, and he expected to be rewarded. Smith had once been a United States Senator. He wanted to be one again, and there was a vacancy to be filled.

In those days the election law provided that United States Senators be nominated in the primary elections or by petition to the legislature and then elected by the legislature. Smith's ambition had never been a secret, but during the campaign he had stayed out of the primaries for fear of hurting Wilson's chances. In the same primary election James E. Martine of Plainfield had received a big popular vote for the senatorial seat. Martine was quite clearly the choice of the voters. But now that the Democrats were in power in the legislature, Smith saw a chance of getting to Washington, and he began to put pressure on the brand-new governor.

Wilson had a covenant with the people, he reminded Smith. He had been elected on the promise, among others, that he would not be a tool of any machine. The Democratic Party in New Jersey had just received a vote of confidence from the public. Did Smith want to betray that trust immediately on taking office?

Smith only smiled with amusement, and Wilson was outraged.

Wilson had learned a great deal about politics from his defeat at the hands of the crafty West in Princeton. He did not intend to allow himself to be defeated again. There wasn't much time, because the legislature was to convene in January.

"There is nothing for it but to fight him openly and to a finish," Wilson wrote to a friend.

By "openly" he meant huge public meetings where the electorate could come to learn of their own state affairs; and he meant consulting with Democratic members of the legislature.

The newspapers took up the Martine-Smith story and raised the question: Is Governor Wilson a tool of the machines after all? Voters sent a snowstorm of letters to the governor and the legislators on this question.

In January Governor Wilson won a decisive victory. Both houses elected Martine by a big majority, and Wilson's national star rose still higher.

His next step as both governor and leader of his party in New Jersey was to work with legislative leaders for much needed reform legislation. That same session of the legislature made reforms in the election laws to give the people direct primaries and to require the campaign committees of all candidates to render financial accountings. It enacted laws to prevent corrupt practices in elections. The legislature passed a law establishing a public utility commission to regulate rates and improve service, as well as a workmen's compensation law.

When it adjourned in April the legislature could look back with deep satisfaction upon one of the finest records ever made by a state government. Many found it hard to believe that such a flood of reforms had taken place in so few weeks.

At Sea Girt that summer, the Wilsons found themselves the center of admiring visitors most of the time, not to mention quantities of persons who wanted to ingratiate themselves and be on the winning side in case Wilson became President. One genuine convert to the Wilson camp was Joe Tumulty of Jersey City, and by the time the Martine-Smith battle was over he had become Wilson's personal secretary. Good-natured and tactful, the short and sturdy Irishman proved a tremendous help in sorting out people and arranging appointments.

Naturally, Wilson's second year as governor did not go as smoothly as his first. No one could accomplish so much without making enemies, and the Essex County Democratic machine wanted his scalp. In the 1911 elections the Republicans showed surprising strength. From then on Governor Wilson had to work hard to get bills through the legislature, and he was not always successful.

At the same time Wilson-for-President clubs were springing up like mushrooms all over the United States, and one day toward the end of 1911 a tall, handsome, progressive Democrat from New York State called on Governor Wilson. His name was Franklin Delano Roosevelt, and he had recently been elected to the New York State Senate from a traditionally Republican district. He was a cousin of Republican Theodore Roosevelt.

The former university president enjoyed talking to

young men, particularly when they had as much energy and enthusiasm as this fellow. Twenty-eight-year-old Roosevelt was convinced that Wilson ought to be the next Democratic candidate for the Presidency.

"How many New York delegates to the Democratic National Convention would there be for me?" Wilson asked.

"About thirty out of the ninety," Roosevelt told him, "but because of the unit rule the block of ninety will be anti-Wilson until released."

Wilson smiled. Roosevelt was sure he could strengthen Wilson's support in New York State and that when the delegates were released by New York's candidate they would switch to Wilson. After taking his leave of Governor Wilson, Senator Roosevelt returned home to help organize the New York State Wilson Conference.

All over the country men, who had heard Wilson lecture, who had gone to school with him, who had read his books, or who had been among his students, were catching fire with the idea of Wilson-for-President. Pleasant Stovall, a playmate in his Augusta days, was now editor of the *Savannah Evening Press* and a Wilson supporter. William Cabell Bruce, who had once debated with Wilson as an undergraduate, was another fan. Heath Dabney could hardly contain himself for joy, and Richard E. Byrd was heading up the Wilson movement in Virginia. Cleveland H. Dodge was donating large amounts of money for a mail campaign. And there was Walter Page, by now editor of the *World's Work* and co-founder of Doubleday, Page & Company, and, of course, George Harvey of *Harper's*.

During 1911 and 1912 Wilson did a great deal of traveling to vital areas to win delegates to his own support, and one of the first cities that he visited was Atlanta, Georgia, where he had once been a penniless young lawyer. Judge George Hillyer, who had then examined Wilson for admission to the bar, was chairman of the meeting at which he spoke, and in his introduction called Governor Wilson the "man who is going to be President of the United States."

While he was still in Atlanta he received a telegram from Ellen urging him to come straight home and not dawdle at any other meetings, because she had arranged a meeting between him and William Jennings Bryan.

Woodrow Wilson chuckled when he read the telegram, because Ellen was becoming a better politician than he. She knew that Bryan was the leader of the national party and that no candidate could hope for the nomination without his approval. When she heard that Mr. Bryan was speaking in Princeton she invited him to dinner. Bryan accepted, because he was just as curious about Wilson as Wilson was about him. Bryan's *Commoner* had carried a big article praising Wilson's achievements as governor, and Ellen's hopes were high.

The two prominent men had been growing toward each other in their thinking, although they never agreed on everything. Both men were of high integrity, both were religious, both were brilliant.

Bryan, Wilson had learned, was a pacifist. This stirred his own recollections of the Civil War in Georgia and the Reconstruction years in South Carolina, and his feelings that war is a kind of barbarism that mankind cannot afford. Mankind was beginning to realize it. The Hague Peace Conference a decade ago had indicated that, and the Czar had called a Second Hague Peace Conference in 1907.

When Governor Wilson and Mr. Bryan met they liked each other at once, and as they sat at the table in the dining room of the Princeton Inn they grew cordial and gay, competing in telling humorous stories. Bryan thought that Ellen, Jessie, and Eleanor Wilson were absolutely lovely. Wilson thought Bryan had "extraordinary force of personality . . . a truly captivating man."

After that evening affair Joe Tumulty clasped Ellen's hand warmly and said, "Mrs. Wilson, you have as good as nominated your husband for the Presidency."

Many others felt so, and wanted to organize a formal campaign committee. William F. McCombs, Princeton graduate and New York attorney, became Wilson's campaign manager.

The first step the committee planned was a speaking tour to the West Coast, starting in Philadelphia. It proved a nerve-wracking experience; Wilson had to answer endless questions from reporters, pose for news photographers wherever he went, wave heartily to crowds, make long train trips, and arrive appearing fit and fresh, ready to talk to any kind of audience, cultured and uncultured, friendly and unfriendly.

Many states had their own favorite sons. The strongest was Champ Clark of Missouri, well known as Speaker of the House of Representatives. Alabama had Congressman Oscar W. Underwood. Ohio had Governor Judson Harmon, who was opposed to Bryan. These were all men with long records in public office and big followings.

When Governor Wilson reached Missouri, he met far more enthusiasm than he had hoped for, and from there he went on to Denver, Colorado, to discover that he was scheduled to speak on Sunday evening. But he had made it entirely clear that he made no political speeches on Sunday! On Sunday *he* went to church. His managers assured him that his talk was to be on the Bible and that many churches were canceling their evening services so that their congregations could hear Mr. Wilson. Under those circumstances he consented.

With almost no preparation, Woodrow Wilson addressed an audience that packed the municipal auditorium. He had never spoken with deeper inspiration, and when he finished his audience knew that he could not know his Bible so well if he did not read it every day, and they knew that his faith was his way of life.

The oftener Wilson spoke, the more convincing and

eloquent he became; and he was always the man who would not compromise with principle, the liberal, the progressive Democrat. He favored tariff reforms downward, election reforms to give people more voice in their own government, world peace, improved working conditions for labor; and he had already proved in his Princeton battle that he opposed placing control in the hands of a few wealthy men.

He spoke in Bryan's home state of Nebraska, in the three Pacific states, and then returned home through the South, stopping at Columbia, South Carolina, and then coming northward to Raleigh, North Carolina. He particularly wanted to visit Josephus Daniels, editor of *The News and Observer,* in Raleigh.

Josephus Daniels was a friend and admirer of Bryan's and a Democratic National Committeeman, and he and Woodrow Wilson had met more than two years before, in January 1909, when Wilson was in North Carolina to speak at the celebration of the hundredth birthday of Robert E. Lee. By the time of Wilson's pre-convention speaking tours, they were friends, and Wilson stayed at the Daniels's home. Editor Daniels became one of Wilson's most able publicity men.

Woodrow Wilson finished up his tour in Washington, D.C., for a conference with McCombs, Page, and Tumulty. It was time, they agreed, to rent office space and open official campaign headquarters, and two more important figures joined the dedicated group: William Gibbs McAdoo and Edward Mandell House.

McAdoo was born in Georgia, and by the turn of the century he was a successful attorney in New York City. He and Wilson had been friends since the latter's days as president of Princeton, when one of McAdoo's sons had been a student there. Like Wilson, McAdoo had creative vision, and when he became irked by delays on the ferry boats crossing the Hudson River, he conceived the idea of a tunnel under the river. In less than four years of work he brought into being the Hudson Tubes, the Hudson Terminal Building, and the Hudson and Manhattan Railroad Company. McAdoo, tall, slender, keen-minded, was the persistent and determined type.

Colonel House, on the other hand, was short and frail in health, and looked like anything but the Texan that he was. He was an independently wealthy man, deeply interested in politics, and a power in the Democratic Party in his state, where he launched the Wilson-for-President campaign.

Because he had heard so much about Governor Wilson from men like McCombs and McAdoo, Colonel House invited Governor Wilson to call on him at his hotel while he was in New York. Wilson accepted the invitation, and in November, 1911, spent an hour with the man from Texas. They would have talked longer, but the governor had another appointment to keep.

"The first hour we spent together proved to each of us that there was a sound basis for a fast friendship," Mr. House wrote later.

They met often after that, and in a very few weeks Colonel House remarked to Governor Wilson:

"We have exchanged confidences which men usually do not exchange except after years of friendship."

"My dear friend, we have known one another always," Wilson replied.

By the end of 1911 the Wilson family was living in a whirlwind. Their suite at the Princeton Inn was so inadequate that they had to rent a house on Cleveland Lane in Princeton. The whirlwind spun faster as the anti-Wilson men, Mr. Smith of Essex in particular, went into action. Princeton trustees and graduates who had opposed Wilson on the graduate-school controversy came out against him again. The Hearst papers criticized him without mercy. The *New York Sun,* a conservative Republican paper, managed to obtain the letter in which Wilson had written—almost five years ago!—that he would like to see Bryan knocked into a cocked hat. The *Sun* published it in the January 7, 1912, issue. The plot: to break up the Wilson-Bryan team.

As a matter of fact, Bryan was visiting at the home of Josephus Daniels in Raleigh, when a reporter from the *Sun* appeared to get a statement from Bryan about the matter.

The moment was tense. Daniels held his breath to see whether Bryan would turn against Wilson.

"You may wire the *Sun,"* Bryan growled, "that you have seen Mr. Bryan and he said that if Mr. Wilson wants to knock him into a cocked hat, Wilson and the *Sun* are on the same platform. That's what the *Sun* has been trying to do to him since 1896."

The reporter withdrew with his statement. At the Jackson Day Dinner in Washington soon after, Bryan deliberately posed for the cameras with his arm around Wilson, and that was the end of that crisis. Wilson never forgot Bryan's forgiving and generous act.

By the time the Democratic National Convention began to convene in Baltimore in June, the Wilson family had moved to their summer place at Sea Girt, and the house was a beehive. If ever the Democratic Party had a chance to capture the Presidency, this was the year! The Republican National Convention had just renominated the ultraconservative Taft, and progressive Republicans, led by the enraged and storming Teddy Roosevelt, were threatening to form a third party, splitting the Republican vote in two. All good Democrats hoped that it would happen.

As a candidate for the nomination, Governor Wilson could not in good taste attend the convention, but he had a direct wire connection from Sea Girt to McComb's office in Baltimore, where men like Josephus Daniels, William Jennings Bryan, William Gibbs McAdoo, young Franklin Delano Roosevelt were working for him. At his side in Sea Girt sat Joe Tumulty. Colonel House had gone to Europe to recover from a bout of illness.

Interest was tremendous in the Sea Girt region, and

newsmen were literally camped on the lawn—in tents —jotting down every fragment of news as it came in from Baltimore.

There was no radio, only the vibrating telephone wires and messengers running back and forth with telegrams. The news came in bits and pieces, maddeningly brief, and Governor Wilson and his secretary lived in constant tension. They knew that Baltimore in June is hot and humid, that Convention Hall was packed with hundreds and hundreds, smoking, sweltering, excited, and they did their best to be patient.

First a temporary chairman had to be chosen, and each faction wanted the advantage. Bryan went hard after the post for the man of his choice, but he lost out to the conservatives. A defeat for Bryan meant a defeat for Wilson. The situation really was not hopeful. Champ Clark had run "like a prairie fire" in the primaries, bringing in such big states for him as Illinois, Massachusetts, California, Bryan's Nebraska, and, of course, his own state of Missouri. Judson Harmon and Oscar W. Underwood each had big followings. Underwood had beaten Wilson in both the Georgia and Virginia primaries.

Woodrow and Ellen Wilson were remaining calm, and they had been talking of a vacation in the British Isles as soon as his term of governor expired. They particularly wanted to see Rydal Mount again.

Soon the news came in that Bryan had won the permanent chairmanship, and the solemn-faced Joe Tumulty began to brighten. He grew brighter with each passing hour.

"Newton Baker mentioned your name in a speech and it has touched off a demonstration," he reported. Half an hour later, the telephone still in his hand, Tumulty shouted joyously, "It's still going on! It isn't over yet!"

The convention had opened on Tuesday; on Thursday it was still on preliminaries with no hope of nominations in sight, when Bryan came to the speaker's desk. Bryan was the most conspicuous figure at the convention, and probably one of the most popular. He was used to the limelight, an automatic speechmaker, always ready to roar out dramatic statements. But his good or bad judgment could win or lose Wilson the nomination, and his judgment was not always good.

The heavy-set crusader, his long hair turning silver, the man who had made the famous Cross of Gold speech, introduced a daring resolution. It opposed the nomination of any candidate obligated to the millionaires J. P. Morgan, Thomas F. Ryan, and August Belmont, or any other member of the privilege-hunting and favor-seeking class; and a further resolution to banish from the convention any delegates representing them.

The convention gasped. Joe Tumulty at his telephone in Sea Girt hoped Wilson would believe what he was being told. The convention went into a shouting pandemonium. The Wilson household huddled around the telephone. The crowds on the lawns pushed closer to the house, up onto the porch, some even into the living room, to hear what the convention would do with Bryan's resolution, with Bryan, with Bryan's candidate.

"Bryan has gone round the bend," was the thought in many minds.

But Bryan hadn't at all. The convention adopted the first half of his resolution, known today as the "anti-Wall Street Resolution," and William Jennings Bryan emerged stronger and more influential than ever, still the melodramatic leader of the progressive wing.

That same evening an already tired convention began to hear nominations of candidates for the Presidency. At last! This was it!

First came the name of Oscar W. Underwood of Alabama, a long speech and a demonstration, seconding speeches and demonstrations. Next came Champ Clark's name, speeches, and demonstrations. Not until 3:25 o'clock on Friday morning did the roll call reach Delaware. Delaware yielded to New Jersey.

Judge John W. Wescott of New Jersey came forward to place Woodrow Wilson's name in nomination, but the mention of Wilson's name touched off a demonstration so wild that Judge Wescott was unable to utter a word for more than an hour.

Tumulty in Sea Girt, still clinging to his telephone, was almost weeping for joy, but the candidate had gone to bed. His wife and three daughters managed to stay awake long enough to know that his name was placed in nomination, and then they too fell into bed.

But in Baltimore there was no sleep for party workers. A group in the gallery of Convention Hall was chanting, "We want Wilson! We want Wilson!" There were eight candidates in all, and not until seven o'clock in the morning was the first ballot taken:

Clark 440½
Wilson 324
Harmon 148
Underwood 117½

Then there had to be ballot after ballot, ballot after ballot, with constant behind-the-scenes conferring, arguing, persuading. Joe Tumulty went into a depression when he learned that New York's ninety votes had been switched to Champ Clark.

On Saturday morning McCombs telephoned to Wilson and advised him to withdraw his name, and Wilson promptly sent the necessary telegram releasing his supporters. But the phone rang a second time. It was McAdoo begging Wilson to reconsider, to stay in the fight. Wilson agreed to remain in it a little longer.

Slowly the tide began to turn, minor candidates began to drop out. Wilson gained votes, a few here, a few there; Clark lost slowly. Just before adjournment for Sunday, on the twenty-sixth ballot, Clark had 463½ votes and Wilson, 407½.

All day Monday the balloting went on, and by Tuesday Wilson moved into the lead. Soon the big block of

Michigan votes switched from Clark to Wilson, and on the forty-third ballot Joe Tumulty shouted:

"Illinois has switched!"

And again a little later: "The Virginias are in line!"

On the forty-sixth ballot Alabama and Ohio joined the Wilson bandwagon.

It was late in the afternoon on the second of July when Governor Wilson heard the news of his nomination. Steeling himself to be calm in a house filled with delirium, he put down the phone and said to Ellen, "Well, dear, we won't go to Rydal after all."

Outside a brass band began to play, "Hail to the Chief" and "The Conquering Hero Comes."

Woodrow Wilson stepped out onto the big front porch to greet the cheering throngs and thank them.

A month later in his acceptance speech Woodrow Wilson said, "We stand in the presence of an awakened nation, impatient of partisan make-believe." This coming campaign, he assured his listeners, would not be a mere personal contest. It would be based upon "the people's cause." Public officeholders were "servants of the people, the whole people. . . . I feel that I am surrounded by men whose principles and ambitions are those of true servants of the people. I thank God, and will take courage."

10. The New Freedom

OTHERS took courage from Woodrow Wilson. Prominent men who had not met him before his nomination came to Sea Girt to inspect his personality for themselves, and went away filled with confidence and enthusiasm. One of these was Samuel Gompers, president and one of the founders of the American Federation of Labor.

Governor Wilson did not want to scatter his campaign shot by trying to make speeches on every issue, and so he and his campaign managers agreed that he would concentrate on one or two. But voters, and special interest groups, demanded to know where he stood on every issue, during question-and-answer periods, during press interviews. Governor Wilson knew they were entitled to know, and so he spoke the truth.

Negro leaders were afraid that he would take a vindictive attitude toward them, since he was a Southerner. They called on him and learned that he was anything but vindictive. He admitted that he was not ready for integration of the two races, but half a century ago that was not a shocking statement.

Groups working for world peace had no trouble endorsing Woodrow Wilson, but women's groups knew he took a dim view of woman suffrage. Suffrage was a subject about which his views would change in later years, but in those days Ellen Wilson was his ideal for all women: gracious, gentle, gifted, and devoted, willing to let him cast one vote for the entire family.

He had some dark thoughts about the votes his forthrightness was costing him, but his wife and daughters, and others who attended meetings where he spoke and watched audience reactions, knew his honesty was winning him more votes than it was costing him.

Eleanor, the youngest, said, "He did not realize how much his personal traits contributed to his success, both as an educator and as a statesman. Direct and frank, lucid and balanced, he inspired confidence. His whole manner was in sharp contrast with the empty bombast and devious palaver of the familiar type of political candidate."

Woodrow Wilson did not know the answer to all the questions that were bothering American voters, and he admitted it frankly. What man could know everything? When he wanted to learn about a subject he consulted someone or several who did know about it. That was how his friendship began with Louis D. Brandeis. Mr. Brandeis was a lawyer and an expert on monopolies. Ellen invited him to luncheon at Sea Girt, and the two men talked all afternoon about the question that so puzzled Governor Wilson: How can we prevent the abuses of private monopolies without creating government monopolies?

"I don't want the American economy enslaved by a few wealthy czars," he said gravely, "but I don't want government regulation that will enslave us."

Mr. Brandeis nodded, and during the weeks ahead loaned Governor Wilson many of his private papers to study. Wise regulation was perfectly possible, he advised, so that small business could compete with large and so that the public would not have to pay unreasonable prices for necessities.

It was already August when Mr. Brandeis came to Sea Girt, and the campaign must begin on Labor Day. Colonel House and his family had returned from Europe, and Governor Wilson was delighted to have this new and completely trusted friend working with him. He asked McCombs to be his campaign manager, with William Gibbs McAdoo as vice-chairman.

McCombs was devoted to Woodrow Wilson, but he was tense and rather erratic, and jealous of McAdoo. Many important party men disliked him. As a result of his own nervous tensions and overwork at the Baltimore Convention, McCombs suffered a complete breakdown around the middle of August, leaving McAdoo in command to practically everyone's satisfaction.

But Woodrow Wilson was the real mastermind of

his own campaign. He began it in Buffalo with a stirring speech to union men on Labor Day and carried it on in city after city.

From the beginning of his campaign Wilson talked of a new kind of freedom for the American people. He stood for freedom from the wrongs that still existed in the American system, particularly for freedom from its control by a very small number of persons:

"The treasury of America does not lie in the brains of the small body of men now in control of the great enterprises that have been concentrated under the direction of a very small number of persons. The treasury of America lies in those ambitions, those energies, that cannot be restricted to a special favored class. It depends upon the inventions of unknown men, upon the originations of unknown men, upon the ambitions of unknown men. Every country is renewed out of the ranks of the unknown, not out of the ranks of those already famous and powerful and in control. . . . We are upon the eve of a great reconstruction."

He did not spare himself. His speaking tours took him to almost every part of the United States, to the West, to New England, to the South. The weeks of September and October were probably the most strenuous and exhausting of his life. His neuritis sometimes bedeviled him; his digestion went back on him. Because he had to shake hands with so many thousands of people, he was afraid that his right hand would become crippled again, and so he developed the habit of holding it with the fingers hanging down limp into the other person's hand.

This was why William Allen White, editor of the *Gazette* in Emporia, Kansas, had said of Wilson: "When I met him, he seemed to be a cold fish. I remember I came home from the meeting at Madison, Wisconsin, and told Mrs. White that the hand he gave me to shake felt like a ten-cent pickled mackerel in brown paper—irresponsive and lifeless."

Editor White liked Wilson's record as governor of New Jersey, but his political sympathies were with the third party that Theodore Roosevelt and other progressive Republicans had started, The Progressive Party, or "Bull Moosers" as they were nicknamed, with Teddy Roosevelt as their Presidential candidate. Many of TR's ideas were as progressive as Wilson's. Optimists were sure that TR would merely divide the Republican vote, that the American people were tired of his booming voice and melodramatics. But others felt that he would draw support from the progressives in both parties, and if he did that he could win the election. And there was the additional argument that he had already had experience as President preceding Taft.

Taft simply did not have audience appeal, and so the two stars of the campaign were Roosevelt and Wilson.

Wilson was at home in Cleveland Lane, having a

brief rest and conferences with McAdoo, Colonel House, Tumulty, and others, when he received the shocking news that Theodore Roosevelt had been shot by a fanatic while making a campaign speech in Wisconsin.

Ellen gasped at the possibility of the same thing happening to Woodrow. Everyone concerned insisted at once that he have a bodyguard.

"Nonsense!" was his reply. He would hear of no such thing.

Colonel House was a Texan. He sent a telegram to a Texan friend, retired Captain Bill McDonald of the Texas Rangers: "Come immediately. Important. Bring your artillery."

When the tall, husky bodyguard arrived, wearing a pair of six-shooters, Woodrow Wilson was furious. He was not interested in hearing that Captain McDonald could hit the eye of a mosquito at fifty paces.

His fury was ignored, and he had to resign himself to Captain McDonald's company for the balance of the campaign.

Woodrow Wilson wrote a letter of sympathy to his opponent, and as soon as TR had recovered he and Wilson were on the road once more.

Both men wound up their campaigns in New York City at Madison Square Garden. TR was there on October 30, speaking to cheering, shouting, whistling throngs, and Governor Wilson was there the next night. The Wilson tide had been rising, and when he and

Mrs. Wilson appeared on the platform the mob went wild with yelling and stamping, waving banners. The ovation went on for over an hour. This was their winner, their new party head, and this was their year to win the election.

On Election Day the Wilson family waited quietly at the house on Cleveland Lane. In the afternoon William Gibbs McAdoo and Josephus Daniels, Joe Tumulty, and one or two more joined them. Through supper and the long evening they waited together, while Governor Wilson read to them from the poems of Robert Browning, and crowds of newsmen waited on the porch.

At ten o'clock that night a message was brought to Mrs. Wilson. She read it, turned to her husband and laid a hand on his shoulder. "My dear," she said in a voice that was almost a whisper, "I want to be the first to congratulate you."

He held her hands a moment in silence.

In another instant pandemonium broke forth. The bells of Princeton University tolled joyously. Students formed a torchlight parade and rushed to Cleveland Lane. Friends, reporters, crowds filled the house.

Loving hands rushed the new President-elect to the front porch where a huge crowd was clamoring for a speech.

It was difficult for him to speak, but as soon as he could control his voice, he said:

"I summon you for the rest of your lives to work to

set this government forward by processes of justice, equity and fairness. I myself have no feeling of triumph tonight. I have a feeling of solemn responsibility."

Ellen took a gayer view of the victory. With sparkling eyes she later said to her young sister, Margaret Axson, "Did you ever hear of the girl who rejected an offer of marriage from the young George Washington? Many years afterward she stood in her garden and watched him drive past on his way to be inaugurated as first President of the United States. It is said that she fainted dead away and had to be carried indoors and revived. I rather suspect that Woodrow's cousin [Hattie] has often come near to fainting!"

When the count was at last in, the year proved indeed a great one for the Democratic Party. It was back in power for the first time in twenty years, with control of both houses of Congress.

Woodrow Wilson saw the Presidency as a profound responsibility in leadership. As a young man he had written in *Congressional Government* that the office had deteriorated to a weak state and that the strength of the government lay in Congress. He no longer thought that. He felt the office of the President was so vital that the man who held it must be strong. A stronger man than President McKinley could have prevented the war with Spain. Theodore Roosevelt had been a strong and effective President. Wilson did not agree with all of TR's ideas and methods, but he felt that TR had made a considerable contribution in helping to bring about the Second Hague Peace Conference, in launching the construction of the Panama Canal, in modernizing the United States Navy.

Woodrow Wilson was taking up the reins of a leadership that was both national and international, because as the United States grew stronger her relations with other nations would grow closer and more influential. For this reason alone, he must appoint the best possible Cabinet of Presidential advisers. He particularly wanted Colonel House in his Cabinet, but Colonel House declined.

After long conferences with Congressional and party leaders Wilson completed his Cabinet. William Jennings Bryan became his Secretary of State; William Gibbs McAdoo, his Secretary of the Treasury; Josephus Daniels, his Secretary of the Navy. This was the point at which young Franklin Delano Roosevelt came into the national government. Since each member of the Cabinet had an assistant secretary to take care of his mountain of desk work, Josephus Daniels asked FDR to become his Assistant Secretary of the Navy.

The incoming President must also appoint diplomatic representatives to other countries, and Walter H. Page became his Ambassador to the Court of St. James. He appointed Henry Morgenthau to Turkey and Judge James W. Gerard to Germany.

The day before Inauguration Day, Woodrow Wilson and his family left Princeton on a special train with throngs of neighbors and students to see him off, cheering and singing "Old Nassau." In Washington there were more throngs waiting for a glimpse of the family, not to mention hosts of Secret Service men to protect the person of the President-elect.

As they were driven toward the Shoreham Hotel in their automobile, they heard one excited woman in the crowd shouting, "Which is Margaret? Which is Jessie? Tell me, which is Eleanor?"

The entire family was under a constant barrage of cameras and news reporters, favor seekers and just curious. Eleanor began to feel deeply alarmed for her mother. Mrs. Wilson was showing the strain badly; she walked with a slight stoop that her daughters had not noticed before, and her face had lost its plump pink bloom. The girls made her rest as soon as they reached the hotel, because that same afternoon she must go to the White House for tea with the departing President and Mrs. Taft.

Ellen let her daughters dress her for the tea, arrange her hair, fix her hat.

"Mother, you look perfectly lovely!"

But as soon as Ellen had left, Eleanor broke down and sobbed, "It will kill them—it will kill them both!"

The next morning the Wilson ladies were driven to a rostrum built on the portico of the Capitol. There they sat and watched incoming President Wilson and outgoing President Taft arrive together in an open carriage drawn by four horses. All around them as far as they could see was a mass of eager faces, waiting for the ceremony and the new President's inaugural address.

The Chief Justice of the United States, Edward D. White, holding Ellen Wilson's personal Bible, administered the oath of office, and Woodrow Wilson leaned forward to kiss the page opened to Psalm 119.

He turned to the people waiting to hear his voice, but President Wilson hesitated, seeing something that he did not like. Before the platform on which he stood was an empty area, the crowd held back from it by ropes, to protect the safety of the President.

"Remove the ropes," said the advocate of the New Freedom, "and let the people come forward."

The ropes were lowered and the crowd surged to the very rim of the platform where he stood ready to speak. Among them in the front row was Ellen Wilson. She had left her seat and hurried forward with the crowd, face upturned, because she wanted to be directly in front of her husband and not miss a word he uttered.

"Without you I would not be where I am," he had told her that morning.

To the American people he said, "My fellow citizens: There has been a change of government. It began two years ago, when the House of Representatives became Democratic by a decisive majority. . . . What does the change mean? . . . It means much more than the mere success of a party. . . . We have been refreshed by a new insight into our own life. . . . This is not a day of triumph; it is a day of dedication. Here muster, not the forces of party, but the forces of humanity. Men's hearts wait upon us; men's lives hang in the balance; men's hopes call upon us to say what we will do. Who shall live up to the great trust? Who dares fail to try? I summon all honest men, all patriotic, all forward-looking men, to my side. God helping me, I will not fail them, if they will but counsel and sustain me!"

11. A Moral Tone

"He set a moral tone that permeated his entire administration and enabled it to survive a war and a demobilization without a single really important scandal. His sense of duty alone carried him through dark days and made him ready to risk his life for what he thought were noble causes. But his most striking personal attribute was his certain sense of destiny and his conviction that the right cause would ultimately triumph."

Thus writes Professor Arthur S. Link of Princeton University, today's outstanding scholar on President Wilson.

Wilson's moral tone had begun at once with his appointments, and it continued as Cabinet, diplomats, and Congressmen began to taste the strength of his leadership. He called his Cabinet together the day after his Inauguration and announced that there would be a special session of Congress early in April.

Meanwhile Ellen was settling the family on the second floor—the family floor—of the White House, with the assistance of Irwin H. (Ike) Hoover, Chief Usher, who had been a White House employee for more than twenty years.

The Oval Room would be their sitting room, the family meeting place, and there they had their piano and books, and there Mrs. Wilson stood her easel. In the room designated as the President's private study, Woodrow Wilson had the original bookcase, purchased with the first money he had ever earned.

The girls could each choose a room to her taste.

"My first impression of the bedrooms was that they were terrifyingly large," wrote Eleanor. "They were all in suites, with bedroom, dressing room and bath. The room chosen for Jessie and me had enormous, old-fashioned wardrobes, a marble mantel and great carved gilt mirrors."

That room, or suite, was in the northeastern part. Margaret was studying music, and so she chose a room distant from the others, the one in which Lincoln had signed the Emancipation Proclamation. The President and Mrs. Wilson had a suite on the south side, with a view of the gardens and the Washington Monument.

"My public career must not spoil your lives," President Wilson said to his three daughters. He insisted that Margaret go on with her music, Jessie with her social welfare work, and Eleanor with her painting.

Woodrow and Ellen did their best to follow the kind of private family life to which they were accustomed, having relatives come to visit them for long periods, having song fests in the evening, dining gayly around a big table, listening later while he read aloud to them from their favorite poets.

Gradually they drew others into their family circle. One was the President's personal physician, Rear Admiral Cary T. Grayson, who had also been President Taft's doctor. Dr. Grayson was a genial, mild-mannered man, slightly shorter than Wilson, and with some of Wilson's own personality traits, such as a love of fine books, a keen wit, and a fondness for telling funny stories. The jolly, plump Joe Tumulty was another; he had come to Washington as the President's personal secretary. The most trusted friend of all was still Colonel House.

President and Mrs. Wilson startled the social world almost immediately by announcing that there would be no Inaugural Ball. They both considered it too frivolous, and Ellen Wilson very soon began to devote her spare time to social work. There were some hideous slums right in the national capital that needed to be cleared and rebuilt, and she began talking to this congressman and that about a bill to provide new housing for Negroes.

The next startling piece of news from the new President was his announcement that he intended to appear before Congress in person at its special session to address them on what he considered the number one domestic issue: tariff revision.

No President had done this since John Adams. It

was the time-honored custom for the President to send his message and have it droned by a clerk. As a result very few congressmen bothered to attend, knowing that they could obtain a copy of the message later.

On April 8, 1913, the hall of the House of Representatives was filled with both Representatives and Senators, and the visitors' galleries were packed, when the President made his formal entrance. The vast audience rose to its feet as he bowed slightly and proceeded to the platform, just beneath the desk from which the Vice-President presided.

The moment was rather strained by this breaking of tradition, as everyone waited to hear the President's address.

"Gentlemen of the Congress," he began. "I am very glad indeed to have this opportunity to address the two houses directly and to verify for myself the impression that the President of the United States is a person, not a mere department of the government hailing Congress from some isolated island of jealous power. . . . After this pleasant experience I shall feel quite normal in all our dealings with one another."

The party now in power, he reminded them, had made the American people a promise, and he was here to ask them to fulfill it promptly.

High protective tariffs that shut out foreign goods altogether gave special groups of manufacturers monopolies and privileges that were not good for the American economy in the long run.

"We must abolish everything that bears even the semblance of privilege or of any kind of artificial advantage, and put our business men and producers under the stimulation of a constant necessity to be efficient, economical, and enterprising, masters of competitive supremacy, better workers and merchants than any in the world."

But, he assured his listeners, it would be unwise to rush into these changes with reckless haste. They must be made gradually without upset or confusion.

"We must build up trade, especially foreign trade. We need the outlet and the enlarged field of energy more than we ever did before."

Just a few more words; he thanked them for their courtesy; and the ten-minute speech was finished.

The audience burst into hearty applause.

Ellen had been there, and as they drove back to the White House, she said, "That was the kind of thing Roosevelt would have loved to do, if he had thought of it."

President Wilson laughed heartily.

"Yes, I think I put one over on Teddy."

While congressional committees were busy drafting a tariff bill, the President was occupied with a multitude of other problems. He was consulting with Mr. Louis Brandeis, Representative Carter Glass of Virginia, Chairman of the House Banking Committee, and Robert L. Owen, Chairman of the Senate Banking Committee, on ways and means of reforming and bringing up to date the banking and monetary affairs of the United States. The banking system was out of date and unsafe. Actually, there wasn't any system, just several thousand individual banks, each operating on its own, and no over-all protection to depositors. Public opinion favored banking reform.

By spring the draft of a bill to be known as the Owen-Glass Bill was ready to be studied and discussed by Democratic Party leaders, the President, and his Cabinet. They were far from being all of one mind, but Wilson managed to steer a course and bring a great idea into being as a law.

That great idea, produced by the cooperative thinking of many men, was the Federal Reserve System, establishing twelve Federal Reserve Banks to operate on a nonprofit basis, to hold deposits in reserve that would help to stabilize money and credit throughout the country. It would be administered by a group of carefully chosen men known as the Federal Reserve Board. All national banks would be required to be members and be under its supervision.

By October the new tariff law was ready for the President's signature, and it would bring tariffs lower than they had been in many years.

In December the Federal Reserve Act had passed both Houses of Congress and was on his desk to be signed.

Next, federal land banks were created that would make loans available to farmers at reasonable rates of interest, and free farmers from the grossly high rates that eastern bankers had been charging. After that came the creation of the Federal Trade Commission which was set up to enforce fair trade practices.

All the while he was moving mountains in domestic affairs, President Wilson was beset by crises in America's foreign relations. There was unrest in the Balkan countries of Europe, a revolution in Mexico, problems to be solved regarding the almost complete Panama Canal, questions about the administration of the Philippines acquired from Spain, and complicated relations between the United States and Asian countries.

President Wilson and Secretary of State Bryan often had their differences on such questions as currency, but they were in complete harmony in their desire to maintain world peace. President Wilson was not a pacifist like Bryan, but all of his life he had carried in his memory the war years in Augusta, the devastation he had seen in Columbia, and the tragedies of Reconstruction. For years he had been giving his support to organizations working for world peace.

The California legislature was discussing the passage of a law to discriminate against its Japanese residents, making it illegal for them to own land. The Japanese Ambassador, President Wilson, and Secretary Bryan held some grave conferences on the question. President Wilson appealed to party leaders in California to reconsider. It could lead to war with Japan! Secretary Bryan went to California to talk personally with legislative leaders. His entreaties did no good. Racial prejudice in California was too strong. The bill was passed and signed into law.

Did President Wilson plan to militarize the Philippines and Alaska against possible attack by Japan? he was asked. He shook his head. He, Secretary Bryan, and Secretary of the Navy Daniels were in agreement that it would be an act of aggression. Instead, they would do all they could to ease the bitterness that the Japanese felt.

A few weeks later, on June 29, 1913, the Second Balkan War broke out and lasted to the end of July. The Balkans were an old trouble spot and must be watched carefully. The war was a dispute among small nations, recently liberated from Turkish rule, over their boundaries. The real danger lay in the fact that the major powers of Europe were all interested and meddling.

The world was full of sensitive danger spots, and the most sensitive that President Wilson had to deal with directly during his first year in office was Mexico.

Mexico had been independent of Spanish rule since 1821, but she was still backward economically and burdened by political factions. Changes in governing regimes were frequent. While Wilson was governor of New Jersey, Francisco Madero became President of Mexico, and for two years he struggled to establish a democratic government, with a multitude of petty chieftains and small factions scheming to overthrow him. Less than a month before Wilson's inauguration, Madero was betrayed by one of his own trusted men, General Victoriano Huerta, and murdered. Huerta became dictator of Mexico, and the country plunged into civil war, bloodshed, and confusion.

As President Wilson assumed office Huerta was demanding that the United States government recognize his regime, with much saber-rattling and threats to American investments in Mexico. The American investors pleaded with the United States government to recognize Huerta and protect their interests.

Wilson was shocked by their selfishness. Were the rights and safety of the twenty-five million people of Mexico to be sacrificed to greed? Secretary Bryan stood shoulder to shoulder with him against recognizing Huerta, but the rest of the Cabinet was divided, and there were mixed views in Congress.

It was a particularly testing time for Wilson, because the Mexican crisis was going on while he was working so hard to get his tariff and Federal Reserve bills passed by Congress.

But Wilson was Wilson. He could not do one thing if he believed another. He sent former Governor John Lind of Minnesota to Mexico as his special agent, with instructions to tell Huerta that the United States would recognize only a government based upon the consent of the governed, that he was President of the entire United States and not just a few special interests, that Huerta could expect recognition if he would end all fighting in Mexico and give the Mexican people a genuine election and a chance to choose their own president.

Huerta rejected the offer, but newspapers at home and abroad praised Wilson for his stand.

And his family frankly adored him. After the tensions and responsibilities of a long day, Woodrow Wilson hurried to join his wife and daughters in their private dining room and in the Oval Room around the fireplace in the evening.

He knew that this circle of love would dissolve away from him in the foreseeable future. All of his daughters were grown women, and Jessie was planning to be married in November to Francis B. Sayre, a professor at Williams College. His Secretary of the Treasury, William Gibbs McAdoo, was courting the President's youngest daughter, Eleanor. Secretary McAdoo had been a widower for nearly two years.

Most difficult of all to accept was the advice that Dr. Grayson had given him about Ellen. Her health was failing, and she had been overtaxing herself with the responsibilities of being First Lady: entertaining, public appearances, social work, even keeping up with her art.

Woodrow Wilson did his best to give Ellen restful vacations. Their first summer in the White House he sent his whole family to Cornish, New Hampshire. The quiet summer helped considerably, but Ellen was seriously ill, and Dr. Grayson told the President as gently as he could that she had Bright's disease. Her energy waned slowly but steadily, and Woodrow Wilson watched her decline with an aching heart.

For Ellen's sake they would have preferred a small wedding for twenty-six-year-old Jessie in November, 1913, but they were America's first family, and the whole country was excited and happy about the prospect of a White House wedding. The list of persons who *had* to be invited was staggering. And so it became a national event with a full list of bridesmaids and attendants.

Jessie had to admit that not many couples received as wedding gifts a silver service from the United States Senate and a diamond pendant from the House of Representatives, not to mention music by a Marine Band in scarlet coats, and diplomats in attendance from all over the world.

Woodrow and Ellen did their best to be cheerful about losing Jessie, and the affair did seem to restore Ellen's vitality. But the President had an aching lump in his throat as he watched Ellen adjust Jessie's veil and listened to the familiar and loved Presbyterian service, once spoken for himself and Ellen by his father and her grandfather.

When the bride and groom at last departed for their honeymoon in England, Woodrow was unable to say anything. He just put his arm around Ellen's shoulders and led her away.

"I know it was a wedding, not a funeral," Ellen said

to some of the guests, "but you must forgive us. This is the first break in the family."

It was not to be the last break, though, even while they were in the White House. Eleanor and "Mac" wanted to be married in the spring, and Ellen's health was failing.

But Ellen's great concern was for her husband's health, and often he obeyed Dr. Grayson's advice more to please her than for any other reason. Dr. Grayson wanted him to relax over an occasional game of golf, to take drives in the fresh air, to go to the theater, and to be extremely careful of the types of food he ate so that his poor digestion would not grow worse. President Wilson followed the advice as often as he was able.

For the Christmas season Dr. Grayson accomplished as slick a piece of diplomacy as the State Department had ever done. He convinced President Wilson that he ought to take Ellen to the Gulf of Mexico for a holiday; then he convinced Ellen that the President was in desperate need of a rest and must go away. Thus, both of his patients had a real rest in the resort town of Pass Christian, Mississippi, in the warm air and sun.

Shortly after their return Ellen began to fade again, and on the first of March she took a sharp turn for the worse. She slipped on the floor in her room and fell hard. The fall shook her badly, and she had to remain in bed for many days afterward, even though no bones were broken. Dr. Grayson wasn't at all sure she had slipped, because he realized how rapidly her ailment was advancing.

Worried though he was about Europe, Asia, Mexico, a controversy about toll rates in the Panama Canal, Wilson spent every spare minute at Ellen's bedside. He got up once during every night to look in on her, and he was the first one with her in the early morning. He usually went to his White House study after breakfast to look at mail and await the doctor's daily report.

"How is she, Doctor?"

"I am very sorry to say, Mr. President, that I cannot report any improvement."

Ellen was able to leave her bed for a few weeks, but after her fall she had to discontinue all her activities. She could not even think of planning Eleanor's wedding. The date for the wedding was set for May 7, 1914; Eleanor, "the baby," was only twenty-four and "Mac" was fifty. But Woodrow Wilson was the same kind of parent that his own father had been, allowing his children to make their own decisions about their lives.

Accepting this next break in the family and worried about Ellen, the President had never depended more upon his closest friends. Colonel House, the closest of all at that time, was someone with whom he could think out loud on any political subject, no matter how confidential or delicate. Almost as close were Joe Tumulty and Dr. Grayson. The President depended upon Secretary McAdoo to do his behind-the-scenes work among congressmen. His Secretary of State had such a flamboyant and blustering ego that personal intimacy with him was difficult. Secretary Daniels was much more amiable and sympathetic.

President Wilson took Ellen to White Sulphur Springs, West Virginia, early in April, but a telephone call from Bryan rushed him back to Washington. It was an alarming report on the Mexican situation. He left Ellen in the care of a nurse.

The U.S.S. *Dolphin* was taking supplies aboard at Tampico on the eastern coast of Mexico when some of the unarmed crewmen going ashore in a whaleboat were arrested by Huerta's troops. They were soon released, but the admiral demanded an apology and a twenty-one gun salute without checking with Washington first. Huerta refused, and the President and Cabinet felt that they must uphold their own admiral.

Public excitement had already been roused by previous incidents. In the spring an English mining engineer had been murdered by a rebel leader named Villa, and American troops were patrolling the Texas-Mexico border to protect Texans from border raids. This *Dolphin* incident could be the match to the fuse.

President Wilson called his Cabinet into immediate session and he addressed Congress that same day. As usual he was brief and to the point.

"The incident cannot be regarded as a trivial one. . . . A few days after the incident at Tampico an orderly from the U.S.S. *Minnesota* was arrested at Vera Cruz while ashore in uniform to obtain the ship's mail, and was for a time thrown into jail. . . ."

Such offenses, he reminded the legislators, could grow until something gross and intolerable happened which would lead the United States into armed conflict. The time to take preventive measures was now. General Huerta must be required to apologize.

"I therefore come to ask your approval that I should use the armed forces of the United States in such ways and to such an extent as may be necessary."

Congress plunged into debate.

But between two and three the morning after his speech, Joe Tumulty awoke the President from a sound sleep to tell him that Secretary Bryan and Secretary Daniels both wanted to talk to him on the telephone.

"Mr. President, I am sorry to inform you that I have just received a wireless that a German ship will arrive at Vera Cruz this morning at ten o'clock, containing large supplies of munitions and arms for the Mexicans, and I want your judgment as to how we shall handle the situation."

President Wilson shook himself awake and asked Mr. Bryan if he realized what action by the United States would mean.

"What do you think, Daniels?" President Wilson asked his Secretary of the Navy.

"The munitions should not be permitted to fall into Huerta's hands."

"Daniels," said President Wilson into the telephone, "send this message to Admiral Fletcher: *Take Vera Cruz at once.*"

How far would the taking of Vera Cruz carry the situation? How many nations would be involved before it was done? Was the United States to become a battleground once more?

The bombarding and seizing of Vera Cruz alarmed the whole Western Hemisphere. The ambassadors from the three largest South American countries—Argentina, Brazil, and Chile—called upon the President and asked for permission to act as mediators in the United States–Mexican crisis. President Wilson and his Cabinet consented, and a meeting known as the ABC Conference was planned at Niagara Falls, Canada.

Deeply worried, yet hopeful, Woodrow and Ellen Wilson turned their attention to the second White House wedding. Eleanor's wedding would have to be smaller than Jessie's because of Mrs. Wilson's frailty.

At the ABC Conference the three Latin American countries worked out a solution that prevented war and laid a groundwork for friendly relations among all of the countries of the Western Hemisphere. Mexico was to have a provisional government that would give her a constitution and the political reforms that she needed. Huerta would be deposed in favor of a president of the people's choice. The United States would withdraw her troops and agree to respect Mexican territory.

Of course, Huerta would have none of the plan, but other Mexican leaders accepted it, and in a few months the dictator was deposed and Venustiano Carranza became President of Mexico.

President Wilson wished that he could have resolved the affairs of Europe with mediation conferences. There tensions were increasing, and the danger of a general war was far greater than it had been between Mexico and the United States. In May, 1914, President Wilson asked Colonel House to go abroad and discuss with Ambassador Page in London and Ambassador Gerard in Berlin the increasing animosity.

"Perhaps we can work out a three-way friendship pact among Germany, England, and the United States."

The reports that he was receiving from Colonel House were alarming and depressing. Germany was expanding her armies and her navy, and other European countries, frightened by Germany's "preparedness" program, were rushing to arm themselves. On the twenty-eighth of June, when Colonel House was in Berlin trying to work out a mutual financial program for the three countries plus France, Archduke Francis Ferdinand, heir to the throne of Austria-Hungary, and his wife were assassinated at Sarajevo, a Balkan town near the Serbian border.

Few people in the United States realized how grave the incident was until Austria-Hungary served an ultimatum upon Serbia. Serbia earnestly offered to have the case heard by the Hague Tribunal, but Austria-Hungary declared war on the little nation before the offer could even be considered. Russia began to mobilize her troops; so did France.

These last days of any hope for peace in Europe were Ellen Wilson's last days of life. Dr. Grayson and consulting physicians knew by the summer of 1914 that there was no chance of her recovery, and to Dr. Grayson once more fell the difficult task of telling the President.

Woodrow Wilson was in his office when Dr. Grayson came in. Sitting in the visitor's chair, he told the President as well as he could.

Wilson's face filled with anguish, and for the next few moments he could not face affairs of state.

"Let's get out of here," he said to Dr. Grayson, and together they walked about in the gardens behind the White House. At last the President sank down upon a bench and reached the bottom of despair.

"What am I to do!" he cried.

But in another instant the tough, covenanting Scot in him asserted itself, and he sat up straight and said, "We must be brave for Ellen's sake."

Rising, he strode back into the White House and upstairs to Ellen's room, and from then on he spent as much time as he could at her side. He even brought his work to her room at times and drafted letters as he sat with her.

On the first of August Germany declared war on

Russia; two days later she declared war on France, and when she marched troops through neutral Belgium to attack France, Great Britain declared war on Germany.

Sitting at Ellen's side, Woodrow Wilson composed a message to the countries of Europe, offering the services of the United States in mediating their difficulties.

Soon thereafter he issued a proclamation of United States neutrality. That was the fifth of August, Ellen's last day but one. The President went to her room every moment that he could find between Cabinet conferences and diplomatic meetings. The United States must be kept out of this holocaust. Ellen must not be denied any comfort he could give her.

Jessie Wilson Sayre and her husband arrived at the White House. Eleanor Wilson McAdoo and "Mac" were there, and Margaret was at home. Stockton Axson was on his way east from Oregon.

On the morning of August 6, 1914, Joe Tumulty canceled all of the President's appointments, because Ellen Wilson was sinking rapidly. There was nothing to do but wait, in that big tomblike place. Word was received that her wished-for bill for slum clearance had been hurried through both Houses of Congress so that she could hear the good news, and she did manage a smile for that.

At last, about five in the afternoon, with her family around her, the President holding her hand, Ellen whispered, "Please take good care of Woodrow, Doctor," and slipped away. She was only fifty-four.

Woodrow Wilson folded her hands gently across her breast and stepped back. Then, and only then, did his iron reserve break, and he sank down and sobbed.

Two days later he rode with her in a private Pullman car to her home town, Rome, Georgia, and there she was buried near her parents.

When President Wilson arrived back at the White House he recalled a conversation he had had with outgoing President Taft on the day of his own Inauguration.

"I'm glad to be going," President Taft had said. "This is the loneliest place in the world."

12. The Idea of America

WOODROW WILSON returned to the darkest, loneliest hours of his life.

On his desk waited a mountain of correspondence, bulletins from Europe, confidential messages from his ambassadors in England, Germany, France, Italy. Trade with belligerents was being cut off, just as the new tariff law was making increasing trade possible. The financial structure of America could be wrecked by a disrupted world economy.

"Every reform we have won will be lost if we go into this war," he said to Secretary Daniels.

President Wilson's personal grief was still so intense that he acted and thought almost mechanically for a while.

"I never understood before what a broken heart meant, and did for a man," he confided to a friend. "It just means that he lives by the compulsion of necessity and duty only and has no other motive force. Business, the business of a great country that must be done and cannot wait, the problems that it would be deep unfaithfulness not to give my best powers to, because a great people has trusted me, have been my salvation."

Close to him to give him what comfort they could were his unmarried daughter, Margaret, now twenty-eight, who became his hostess at the White House, Dr. Grayson, Joe Tumulty, and closest of all Colonel House, who had returned from Europe just before the outbreak of the war. Helen Bones, a cousin, who had come to the White House as Ellen's personal secretary, remained to assist Margaret.

For the first few weeks after Ellen's death Woodrow Wilson was closest to the Texan, Edward M. House.

"Mr. House is my second personality," the President said. "He is my independent self. His thoughts and mine are one."

They thought aloud together almost as one person, and Wilson shared every confidence with the Colonel.

Almost as close to the President was Ellen's brother, Stockton Axson, who remained at the White House for a while after his sister's death.

One evening Woodrow and Stockton sat chatting quite late, and Dr. Axson, who sensed that the President was struggling to develop an important idea, said as little as possible himself.

"Stock," the President said, "I am afraid something will happen on the high seas that will make it impossible for us to keep out of the war."

Stockton kept silent and waited.

"It is perfectly obvious that this war will vitally change the relationships of nations," the President went on. "Four things will be essential to the re-establishment in the world after peace is made.

"1. No nation shall ever again be permitted to acquire an inch of land by conquest.

"2. . . . a recognition of the reality of equal rights between small nations and great.

"3. Munitions of war must hereafter be manufactured entirely by the nations and not by private enterprise.

"4. There must be an association of the nations, all bound together for the protection of the integrity of each . . ."

The idea of an association of nations to keep peace and arbitrate differences was not new. Scholars had thought of it as far back as the sixteenth century. But the two Hague Conferences showed that the idea was beginning to seem practical to more and more people. Now, this new kind of war, not between two nations, but embroiling the whole world, perhaps even the United States, made it clear that mankind must take measures to prevent such a catastrophe from ever happening again. Those who knew Wilson well knew that he wanted the United States to assume the leadership toward this end. She must do two things: she must take the initiative in bringing about a lasting peace, and she must be firm about her own rights as a neutral under international law. Neutrality must not be mistaken for weakness.

"The idea of America is to serve humanity," President Wilson had said just the previous June to the young men graduating from the Naval Academy in Annapolis.

But America must keep her sabers sheathed; she must remain neutral. This the President fervently believed, and in August he addressed a plea to all of the American people for neutrality in an address to the Senate:

"The effect of the war upon the United States will depend upon what American citizens say and do. . . . The people of the United States are drawn from many nations, and chiefly from the nations now at war. . . . I venture, therefore, my fellow countrymen, to speak a solemn word of warning to you against that deepest, most subtle, most essential breach of neutrality which may spring out of partisanship, out of passionately taking sides . . ."

The President received such a flood of praise from friends, associates, the press, even some political opponents, for his stand on a strong, effective neutrality that his grief-stricken heart felt almost light again. Liberal Republicans like Teddy Roosevelt came out for a "strict neutrality." Conservative Republicans like Senator Henry Cabot Lodge, however, criticized the President severely, declaring the idea of neutrality in the midst of war "unsound" and "impractical."

It was not an easy course to steer. What about loans to belligerent countries? What about orders from them for munitions and food?

Loans and sale of munitions and arms were quickly declared inconsistent with neutrality.

"Money is the worst of contrabands—it commands all other things," wrote Secretary of State Bryan in his *Commoner.*

But food was another matter. Great Britain was blockading German ports even against food supplies in an effort to starve Germany out of the war. When President Wilson tried to persuade both sides to respect the neutrality of United States' unarmed ships on the high seas, both sides grew testy. The Central Powers would if the Allies would. The Allies would certainly not lift their food blockade.

Trade was the knottiest problem of all in 1914 and 1915. The United States had a very meager merchant marine and had depended to a great extent on foreign ships to transport her cargoes. What few private shipowners there were in the United States were suddenly making tremendous profits, transporting cargo. Three hundred per cent profit on a voyage was usual.

President Wilson and Secretary McAdoo went to work, in conference with the party leaders of both Houses of Congress, to draft a shipping bill to appropriate thirty million dollars so that the government could purchase and operate cargo ships. But the ship purchase bill caused a fierce debate in Congress. Lodge led the fight against it in the Senate. Many of the bill's opponents were sincere in their fear that it would be dangerous for the government to go into private business, that it was a move toward socialism, that the President was seeking to increase his personal power. But other objections came from lobbyists working for the private shipping interests, which did not want to lose their excessive war profits. They did not want to compete with government ships charging fair rates.

Wilson felt heartsick at the greed and lack of faith. "Our bountiful crops are ready to harvest. Unless they can be carried to the foreign markets, they will waste in the warehouses, if they do not rot in the fields!"

"President Wilson had his jaw set," was someone's remark; but a set jaw was not enough to accomplish the passage of the ship purchase bill. He and McAdoo argued and reasoned with legislators, with shipowners, with the pressure groups, but to no avail. Even though the bill squeaked by in the House, Henry Cabot Lodge and Elihu Root succeeded in talking it to death in the Senate.

The honeymoon between President and Congress was decidedly over, but in spite of the shipping bill dispute the Democratic Party managed to retain its majority in both Houses in the November, 1914, elections.

Because Woodrow Wilson's own attitude was one of

service and dedication, he felt deeply bitter about the difficulties in trying to accomplish what was best for America. Not only was he still burdened by the loss of Ellen, but there were jealousies and rivalries among the men closest to him and upon whom he depended. Many of the Cabinet members, Bryan among them, were jealous of Colonel House, who was closer to the President than anyone. Others were trying to oust Joe Tumulty because he was a Roman Catholic. Colonel House in his turn disliked Secretary Daniels and was trying to remove him from the Cabinet.

Over all loomed the specter of war that grew larger and more threatening with each passing hour.

Colonel House kept in touch in a confidential, unofficial way with the American ambassadors in Germany, England, and France, and with many of the high foreign officials in Washington and abroad, especially regarding President Wilson's ambition to have America act as mediator and bring the war to an end. Ambassador Page in London was not very sympathetic. He wanted the United States to come into the war on the side of the Allies.

"Civilization must be rescued," Page wrote to House. "There's no chance for it until German militarism is dead."

But there were other factors in the situation. Destroying Germany would make possible the westward expansion of Russia, House reflected. These were the days of "balance of power" politics in Europe.

By the end of 1914, the German armies, which had expected to have France conquered and occupied by then, had suffered a defeat in the battle of the Marne. Their lines that had been within a few miles of Paris were withdrawn to Verdun. The French strength and preparedness had surprised them. And so, as winter weather approached, when military activities would be difficult, Page wrote to Secretary Bryan:

"The military situation is a stalemate. The Germans cannot get to Paris or to Calais."

The men in Europe with whom House was corresponding wanted him to come to Europe and discuss the possibility of working out some sort of peace, and President Wilson gave his consent.

In spite of protests from family and friends about the danger of mines, and the advice of those who considered the mission hopeless, Colonel House sailed on the *Lusitania* on January 30, 1915.

A few days after his arrival in England, Germany announced that she was setting up a blockade around Great Britain. It was to be accomplished with a new and deadly weapon, the submarine. Any enemy merchant ship found within the blockaded area would be destroyed without concern for the lives of passengers or crew, and neutral ships venturing into the zone would be in danger of being mistaken for an enemy.

The news was shocking to Americans who were already becoming pro-Allied in their feelings. Reports of atrocities committed by German armies in Belgium had been fanning public emotions, and the spirit of neutrality was becoming increasingly harder to maintain. The State Department had already eased its ruling about foreign loans, and American bankers were permitted to make private loans to warring nations. Huge amounts of credit were going to the Allies.

America's position must be made clear, if it wasn't already so. President Wilson composed a careful note of warning for the German government, which was dispatched to the American Ambassador in Germany by Secretary Bryan on February tenth. If any "mistakes" were made by German submarines regarding American vessels or lives, said the note, the United States would view the act as "an indefensible violation of neutral rights. . . . If such a deplorable situation should arise, the Imperial German Government" would be held "to a strict accountability for such acts of their naval authorities" and the United States would "take any steps it might be necessary to take to safeguard American lives and property and to secure to American citizens the full enjoyment of their acknowledged rights on the high seas."

Letters from Colonel House contained no hope of a peace settlement. Germany would not consent to withdrawing from Belgium and paying indemnity to the Belgians. Neither side would lift its blockade.

From Paris, House wrote to the President: "I find that the ruling class in France do not desire peace, but that a large part of the people and the men in the trenches would welcome it. This, I think, is also true of Germany."

The two men agreed that freedom of the seas must be upheld. Yet herein lay the danger. Germany had issued an oblique threat to neutral ships.

Woodrow Wilson worked from early morning until late into the night. He worried. He sometimes paced the floor or sat in solitude striving for wisdom.

Dr. Grayson, who checked the President's health every day, realized that there is a limit to how much grief and work and worry any human being can stand. Woodrow Wilson's self-discipline was heroic, but even self-discipline can be overdone.

Dr. Grayson encouraged anything or anyone who could possibly cheer the President, and the first sign of real lightheartedness showed when his first grandchild was born. He looked almost happy again, after so many months, as he sat holding Jessie Wilson Sayre's baby. How white the President's hair was becoming! He was fifty-eight.

The physician particularly insisted that President Wilson have some recreation as often as possible, and they went riding or played golf together. One day as they rode through the park, they passed someone to whom Dr. Grayson nodded; the President asked:

"Who is that beautiful lady?"

That was Mrs. Edith Galt, Rear Admiral Grayson explained, the widow of Norman Galt.

"He was a jeweler here in Washington, and she has

continued to run his business with the assistance of a devoted employee."

Another time Dr. Grayson and the President had just returned to the White House from a game of golf. As they stepped from the elevator they came face to face with Mrs. Galt and Helen Bones. Mrs. Galt was obviously embarrassed, because her friend Helen had assured her that it would be perfectly all right to come to the White House for tea while the President was out playing golf.

Edith Bolling Galt, in her early forties, was extremely beautiful, warm and gracious, with a vitality that seemed to arise from deep within her. Her hair was dark and her eyes were a deep blue-violet. There was a slight Southern drawl to her speech. She was wearing a tailored black suit designed for her by Worth of Paris, and the President wished at once that he were wearing something neater than his sloppy golf togs.

Introductions completed, Helen Bones explained that she had invited Mrs. Galt for tea and asked the President and Dr. Grayson to join them. The two men accepted, and the President hurried to change. They sat for more than an hour before the fireplace in the Oval Room, and then Mrs. Galt took her departure.

Her visit was almost blotted out of Woodrow Wilson's memory by the national and world events that crowded in upon him. Germany was in deadly earnest about her underseas warfare. On March 28 the British-owned ship *Falaba* was sunk and one American passenger drowned. Headlines burst in the American papers. Was Germany to be held "strictly accountable"? If so, was this neutrality? Could America hold Germany accountable and not prepare for war herself?

President Wilson was beginning to realize that Senator Lodge's calling neutrality "impractical" had some justification in it. Yet he must continue to steer a course between the extreme factions at home who cried out for entry into the war on the one hand or were absolute pacifists on the other. Wilson himself wanted peace, but not at any price.

But Mrs. Galt's visit had not been completely blotted out of the President's memory. Feeling desperately alone, he asked Helen Bones to invite Mrs. Galt for a drive and dinner at the White House. It proved to be the quiet, restful kind of evening that he was accustomed to and loved.

"After a quiet little dinner we three sat around the fire and discussed books, and he read aloud several delightful things."

Then, the man who had been so grief-stricken, so cut off from everyone, began to talk to Edith Galt about his family, particularly about his father. He asked Mrs. Galt about herself. She too had been born in Virginia. Her family had been well to do but had lost most of their resources in the Civil War. Like the President, her father had studied law at the University of Virginia.

There could be no forgetting Mrs. Galt after that

evening, not even when he was meeting with his Cabinet on the *Falaba* situation. While they were conferring about the *Falaba* the news came that a German plane had attacked the American steamship *Cushing*.

Woodrow Wilson needed someone to talk to, someone to think aloud in front of, someone he could trust completely. The President of the United States has almost no privacy. At all hours his person must be protected by Secret Service men, and the only people he can be completely alone with are the members of his immediate family. Ellen was gone; two of his daughters were married; he did not have the right to monopolize Margaret. She must go on with her music career and live her own life. And the President of the United States may not make social calls, least of all upon a lady. And so he sent Mrs. Galt a note asking her to call upon him.

The evening was arranged, and Dr. Grayson escorted her in a White House car. Grayson was deeply pleased about this newest development in his patient's life. He considered happiness the best medicine in the world. Edith Galt arrived in a long, black gown wearing the yellow roses that the President had sent her.

The next morning the German Embassy in Washington delivered a warning to the United States that Americans must not enter the war zone around the British Isles except at their own risk.

On the fourth of May the President asked Mrs. Galt to the White House for dinner with Dr. Grayson,

Margaret, Helen Bones, and his sister Mrs. George Howe. After dinner the guests tactfully withdrew and left Woodrow Wilson and Edith Galt alone.

With his usual point-of-the-needle style he told her immediately the purpose of the evening.

"I asked Margaret and Helen to give me an opportunity to tell you something tonight that I have already told them."

He was in love with her, he said, and he wanted her to marry him.

"Oh, you can't love me!" she said in surprise. "You don't really know me; and it is less than a year since your wife died."

"Yes," he said, "I know you feel that; but, little girl, in this place time is not measured by weeks, or months, or years, but by deep human experiences; and since her death I have lived a lifetime of loneliness and heartache."

They talked on until it was time for her to leave, and then the President himself, with Helen Bones, saw her home.

Three days later the British liner, *Lusitania,* was torpedoed and sunk off the Irish coast without any warning to passengers. Nearly 1200 persons died, 124 of them Americans.

It was the match to the fuse of public opinion in America. The sense of horror and repugnance at making war on noncombatants that had been rising burst forth.

"If you do not call her [Germany] to account over the loss of American lives caused by the sinking of the *Lusitania,* her next act will probably be the sinking of an American liner, giving as an excuse that she carried munitions of war and that we had been warned not to send ships into the danger zone," House wrote from London.

He himself returned to America the following month. In his opinion America was no longer a neutral spectator, and President Wilson agreed. He had arrived at the point in his own thinking where he considered neutrality impractical, and he had come to the further conclusion that a preparedness program must be put into effect.

But the most compelling idea in Woodrow Wilson's mind was world peace—a workable, just, enforceable peace—and it had become the great single goal of his life. A lasting peace could be achieved only through some international organization, a league of nations, and he felt that the leadership for this must come from America.

"The idea of America," he had said almost a year ago, "is to serve humanity."

13. The Second Mrs. Wilson

WOODROW WILSON'S changing views on neutrality brought him into deep conflict with his pacifist Secretary of State. While Bryan showed some restraint out of respect for the high position that he held in the government, his attitude in Cabinet meetings was becoming openly hostile toward the President.

That the President was "amazingly considerate" in Cabinet meetings was the opinion of David F. Houston, Secretary of Agriculture: "He is even more amazingly patient and tolerant. I admire his ability to restrain himself at times." But Bryan was beginning to test Wilson's restraint to the cracking point.

Profoundly worried, yet realizing that the utmost in moral strength was needed to carry the country through this crisis with dignity, Woodrow Wilson shut himself up alone for hours to think through every angle of the *Lusitania* crisis and compose a protest to the German government.

"Say exactly what you mean," his father had counseled. "Make your mind like a needle, of one eye and a single point. Shoot your words straight at the target."

The message that Woodrow Wilson read in draft to his Cabinet was directed straight at the target, and after careful consideration and discussion his Cabinet members approved it with only some minor polishing here and there—all except William Jennings Bryan.

"You people are not neutral," Bryan declared. "You are taking sides!"

Other Cabinet members did not agree with him.

"In view of recent acts of the German authorities in violation of American rights on the high seas," said the note, "which culminated in the torpedoing and sinking of the British steamship *Lusitania* on May 7, 1915, by which over a hundred American citizens lost their lives, it is clearly wise and desirable that the Government of the United States and the Imperial German Government should come to a clear and full understanding as to the grave situation which has resulted."

The note went on to review the other sinkings and reminded Germany of the previous statement it had received. This government "must hold the Imperial German Government to a strict accountability for any infringement of those rights, intentional or incidental."

President Wilson could not feel that he was taking sides in this note. He would have addressed the same message to the Allies had they committed this kind of offense.

The note was only the first of three that were sent to Germany about the *Lusitania* incident. Germany claimed that the *Lusitania* had been armed when she had not been, although she was carrying some contraband cargo of munitions. Wilson's second note was stronger than the first, and his Secretary of State, who had signed the first, refused to sign the second. On June 9, 1915, Bryan sent President Wilson his resignation.

"I cannot do otherwise," he confided to Secretary McAdoo.

"Mr. Bryan has resigned as Secretary of State," President Wilson told the Cabinet. "I have, with regret, accepted."

Wilson still had Bryan's letter of resignation in his pocket when he went aboard the *Mayflower* bound for New York to review the Atlantic fleet.

With the President's party aboard the *Mayflower* were two of his daughters, Mr. Tumulty, Dr. Grayson —and Edith Galt. Whatever fragments of leisure the pressures of his office would permit, Woodrow Wilson endeavored to spend with the woman he was courting, and this brief sail down the Potomac and up the coast was one of his precious opportunities.

Family and close friends understood the situation, and they were all growing to love Edith Galt, hoping that she would accept the President's proposal. After dinner everyone went on deck to enjoy the starry mild night and left Edith and Woodrow alone. She took his arm as they strolled along the deck, sensing that he was troubled about something.

"Let's lean on the rail instead of walking, as I want to talk to you," he said, and he told her of Secretary Bryan's resignation.

Having the point of view of the general public, Edith told him her thoughts. Many people, she said, did not take Bryan seriously. To them he seemed more like an actor than a statesman.

"What do you think the effect will be?" Wilson asked her.

"Good," she replied, "for I hope you can replace him with someone who is able and who would in himself command respect for the office both at home and abroad."

He had in mind Robert Lansing, who was already Counselor to the State Department, and they discussed him for quite a while.

After that Edith came to the White House to dinner whenever it was possible to have a private gathering of members of both their families and their friends. With mounting hope he drew her closer and closer into his personal life, and his work was so much a part of his personal life that the two could not be separated. Edith Galt was not only cultured and well educated, but she had sound judgment too. They often talked of affairs of state.

They talked of the way prices were rising in the United States, and the way the economy was beginning to boom, as a result of orders for all sorts of manufactured goods and materials from the Allies.

"Our own loans to them are doing that," he remarked ruefully.

And they discussed the progress of the war in Europe. During 1915 the British and French had launched big offensives against the German line, under the direction of General Joseph Joffre, Chief of the General Staff. The plan was to force Germany out of northern France. But after four major battles the campaign had failed, and the Western Front was about where it had been the year before, after terrible losses. On the Eastern Front the Russian army was losing ground before Austrian and German troops, and morale behind the lines was cracking from lack of munitions, food, and clothing.

German diplomacy had made a stalemate out of the *Lusitania* question, and other sinkings and U-boat attacks continued.

Public opinion was growing rapidly more favorable toward a preparedness program. Prominent men whose opinion influenced the thinking of thousands, editors of big magazines and newspapers, demanded one.

President Wilson asked Secretary of the Navy Daniels and Secretary of War Lindley M. Garrison to draw up a program for increasing the strength of the army and navy. With the guidance of military experts the two departments went to work, and some of the most creative planning for the navy was done by Franklin Delano Roosevelt, the Assistant Secretary.

Wilson took a much needed vacation in Cornish, New Hampshire, in the spacious home of the novelist, Winston Churchill. The house had a wide view of the Connecticut River Valley, and there was an excellent golf course nearby. The house was his for the whole summer, even though he could not be there all of the time.

He had spent other holidays here, but this summer was the most memorable of all. With him were all three of his daughters, Frank Sayre, two grandchildren, Dr. Grayson, and for part of the time, Edith Galt.

Everyone could tell that Woodrow Wilson's suit with Edith was prospering and that she was falling deeper and deeper in love with him. The relaxed country life in New Hampshire, his charm as a parent, were winning her rapidly, and before her visit was over she promised to marry him if he lost the election of 1916. She felt too uncertain of the responsibilities of being First Lady.

But by the first week of September her consent was unconditional, and they began to make plans for their wedding.

By that time he was sharing most of his Presidential problems with her, and when he received the preparedness program that he had asked for he told her how pleased he was with it.

The program recommended expanding the standing force of the regular army by fifty per cent, the building of battleships, cruisers, destroyers, and submarines for the navy, and a similar increase in the number of men in the navy and marine corps.

When he presented it to Congress in December, he urged that the increases in armaments be accomplished with increased taxation to avoid increasing the national debt.

"We have stood apart, studiously neutral," he said in his address. "It was our manifest duty to do so . . . that some part of the great family of nations should keep the processes of peace alive. . . . What we are seeking now, what in my mind is the single thought of this message, is national efficiency and security."

But congressmen could not act with ease unless they had the support of the electorate, and he planned to make a speaking tour of the West to explain his national security program to the people.

By now President Woodrow Wilson was one of the outstanding statesmen of the world. To him had fallen the mission of world leadership, and he was accepting it with his whole heart and soul. He was leading America along a middle road, away from neutrality, not into war as the interventionists would have him do, but into vigorous National Security. He believed this to be a necessary next step toward world order.

Between the time of the sinking of the *Lusitania* and his appeal to Congress for military preparedness funds, a British merchant ship bound for New York with no war materials aboard was sunk without warning. Two Americans died. Wilson and Secretary of State Lansing demanded satisfaction, and this time the German government quailed briefly and promised not to do it again. But a few weeks later the Italian liner *Ancona* suffered the same fate, and more Americans were lost.

These incidents spurred Wilson in his drive for preparedness and in his deep desire for a league to enforce international law after the war. World peace had become the great goal of his life, the goal that brought all of his thoughts into a single focus, that made him into a needle, with one eye and a single point.

Because of this evolving purpose, this change from neutrality to preparedness, his personal popularity was waning throughout the country, he was losing the support of many congressmen, as neutralist groups were deserting him. Many felt that he was showing personal weakness. His popularity was further damaged when his engagement to Edith Galt was announced.

The opposition pounced upon the news of his engagement as an opportunity for a dirty whispering campaign. His wife had been dead little more than a year, they pointed out. He had been untrue to his first wife when she was alive, they whispered. There were *letters!*

Dr. Grayson hurried to the President as soon as he

heard the ugly talk and told him what he had heard. Wilson turned deathly white, and his Scottish jaw set in a hard line.

"There is nothing in any letters I ever wrote that I am ashamed to have published," he declared, and then he added in a low, tragic tone of voice, "Grayson, go and tell Edith everything and say my only alternative is to release her from any promise."

He could not allow her to be exposed to what could develop into a vicious smear campaign.

Woodrow Wilson was a voluminous letter writer, and some of his correspondents were women. What could not his enemies make of that!

Edith Galt immediately wrote him:

"Dearest. . . . I am not afraid of any gossip or threat, with your love as my shield—and even now this room echoes with your voice—as you plead, 'Stand by me—don't desert me!' This is my pledge, dearest one, I will stand by you—not for duty, not for pity, not for honor—but for love. . . ."

When Woodrow Wilson received her letter, his courage failed him completely, and he was afraid to open it for fear of what her decision might be. He slipped it into his pocket. He became so depressed by the turn of events and by the speed with which gossip was spreading that he felt physically sick.

Dr. Grayson watched the President's wretchedness as he strove to carry on affairs of state. He was discussing with House, Lansing, and European diplomats possible approaches to a peace conference. He and McAdoo were drafting a new shipping bill to create a desperately needed modern merchant marine. He and Congressional leaders were planning the National Defense Act that they wanted Congress to put into effect.

But all the while his reputation was being so badly damaged that even within his own party there was talk about nominating someone else in 1916. Wilson's physical condition went down rapidly, because he could neither eat nor sleep. Dr. Grayson, not knowing what Edith's decision had been, went to her and begged her to come to the White House.

"He looks as I imagine the martyrs looked when they were broken on the wheel," he told her. "He does not speak or sleep or eat."

Not realizing that he had not read her letter, Edith Galt hurried to the White House with the doctor and found Woodrow Wilson in bed in a darkened room, "a white, drawn face with burning eyes dark with hidden pain."

She sat down beside him and took hold of his hand, and the misunderstanding was ended. They would be married in December, whatever its effect and whatever the gossipmongers might say.

"If the people do not trust me," said Woodrow Wilson, "now is the time to find out."

Responsible newsmen who knew the President and were sure the gossip was untrue investigated the story carefully. They found that it had been pure invention to damage his chances of re-election.

"The story was made out of whole cloth," wrote David Lawrence.

Edith Galt and Woodrow Wilson were married in her home on Twentieth Street, Northwest, with only closest friends and relatives as guests. The President was fifty-nine, Edith forty-three. They spent the Christmas holidays at Hot Springs, Virginia, as their honeymoon.

The President of the United States may not be out of touch with national and world affairs, even on his honeymoon, and Edith became his intimate assistant right away. She learned to decode messages that came in from abroad, and translated into code the messages that the President wished to send. If he had to work late at night, and he often did, she was beside him at the typewriter.

While they were in Hot Springs plans were completed to send Colonel House abroad once more on a peace mission. Wilson instructed House to go to "several capitals" and present his concern for "the future peace of the world and the guarantees to be given for that. The only guarantees that any rational man could accept, are (a) military and naval disarmament and (b) a league of nations to secure each nation against aggression and maintain the absolute freedom of the seas."

And he added: "If either party to the present war will let us say to the other that they are willing to discuss peace on such terms, it will clearly be our duty to use our utmost moral force to oblige the other to parley . . ."

Woodrow and Edith Wilson returned to the White House early in January, 1916, Edith to become one of the warmest and most gracious First Ladies the nation had had in a long time. She presided capably over huge social affairs, wore beautiful clothes and looked stunning in them, and she had a talent for being completely dignified yet seeming relaxed and gay.

When the President set out on his western tour to explain his preparedness program to the voters, Edith Wilson went with him.

En route from city to city—Cleveland, Milwaukee, Chicago, Des Moines, Kansas City, St. Louis—she became as alarmed as he that people in the Middle West were "almost apathetic regarding the possibility of war."

Wilson did not spare himself in trying to understand and change the apathy that he found.

"America has no reason for being unless her destiny and her duty be ideal," he said in Chicago. "It is her incumbent privilege to declare and stand for the rights of men. Nothing less is worth fighting for, nothing less is worth sacrificing for. . . . therefore, what America is bound to fight for when the time comes is nothing more nor less than her self-respect. . . ."

In Des Moines: "I have spent every thought and energy that has been vouchsafed me in order to keep this country out of war. . . . Yet, there is a price which is too great to pay for peace, and that price can be put in a word . . . self-respect. . . . America can not be an ostrich with its head in the sand. America can not shut itself out from the rest of the world. . . ."

14. America Enters the War

WOODROW WILSON returned from his western tour to read correspondence from Colonel House regarding a permanent covenant of world peace and to lock horns with a contrary Congress.

Colonel House thought it "was reasonably certain we would enter some world agreement having for its object the maintenance of peace"; he found the British were slow to act on most everything. In Germany the government was determined to win the war militarily, but between Germany's navy and Foreign Office "a great controversy is going on . . . regarding undersea warfare." In Paris he found French government officials cordial toward Wilson's plan for a postwar settlement.

But, "I doubt whether a crisis with Germany can long be avoided," House cabled to Wilson early in February.

In Congress, in January, Secretary McAdoo had succeeded in having the new shipping bill introduced;

it was destined for a long debate in both Houses before it was finally enacted into law. When a vacancy occurred in the Supreme Court, President Wilson appointed Louis Brandeis, and this brought on another struggle with the Senate before it approved the appointment.

During the third week of February, 1916, the now famous Battle of Verdun began, when German and French forces faced each other along the Meuse River. The fighting went on, with horrible losses on both sides, through the spring and into June. All the while the war went on at sea, and on the fronts between Austria and Italy and between Bulgaria and Greece.

In the Western Hemisphere, Mexico was in a chaotic state with Venustiano Carranza, Huerta's successor, struggling to stay in power. Pancho Villa, an irresponsible chieftain in northern Mexico, opposed to Carranza, staged a military attack on New Mexico. General John J. Pershing was dispatched with troops to the Mexican border, and with consent from Carranza pursued the bandit into Mexican territory.

Thoughtful statesmen realized that Villa was deliberately trying to provoke war with the United States in the hope of overthrowing Carranza. Carranza's motive in allowing Pershing to pursue Villa into Mexico was to rid himself of Villa at no expense to himself. But Villa knew Mexican terrain better than his pursuers, and he was never captured.

The Mexican situation dragged on for nearly a year

and caused deep rifts in the Cabinet and in Congress, with pressure on Wilson from every direction: to intervene, to wait, to declare war, to keep the peace. Carranza at one point did an about-face and demanded the withdrawal of United States troops from Mexican territory. President Wilson through it all succeeded in keeping the peace and eventually assigned General Pershing to a much more important task.

In the midst of Verdun, preparedness, the Mexican crisis, and difficulties between President and Congress, came the news that the unarmed French channel steamer *Sussex* had been torpedoed without warning.

With utmost self-restraint President Wilson drafted a note to the German government that would leave the door open for discussion, but Secretary Lansing was too outraged to send it.

"The time for writing notes has passed!" he insisted.

Colonel House had returned to the United States full of close-range impressions, and he argued with the President that there could be no avoiding a break with Germany. Germany had no intention of giving up her U-boat campaign. Submarines were her big advantage.

Wilson shook his head. Once the break occurred, he knew, there could be no further hope of mediation, and it would probably mean America's entry into the war.

"The President talks boldly, but acts weakly," said some of his militant critics.

Wilson drew up a note to the German government and made it as strong as he felt he wisely could, and he refused to make it any stronger.

"Unless the Imperial Government should now immediately declare and effect an abandonment of its present methods of submarine warfare against passenger and freight-carrying vessels, the Government of the United States can have no choice but to sever diplomatic relations with the German Empire altogether."

The next day he addressed Congress and laid the whole case before them.

"We owe it to a due regard for our own rights as a nation, to our sense of duty as a representative of the rights of neutrals the world over, and to a just conception of the rights of mankind to take this stand now with the utmost solemnity and firmness."

As he spoke he sensed a returning harmony between himself and the legislative body, and when he had finished the congressmen applauded him heartily. Wilson's unpopularity had passed its low point.

During the first week of May Germany agreed not to torpedo any more unarmed merchant ships without warning. Henceforth, vessels suspected of carrying contraband would be searched first. This was the "Sussex Pledge."

Woodrow Wilson could dare to hope that "moral force" had won a victory, and the public could dare to hope that Wilson's patient diplomacy could keep them out of the war.

His heart lightened, President Wilson addressed a meeting of the League to Enforce Peace, three weeks after the achievement of the Sussex Pledge, and laid before them his dream of a league of nations:

"The nations of the world have become each other's neighbors. It is to their interest that they should understand each other. In order that they may understand each other, it is imperative that they should agree to co-operate in a common cause, and that they should so act that the guiding principle of that common cause shall be even-handed and impartial justice. This is undoubtedly the thought of America . . ."

Early in June Congress passed the National Defense Act, making a great part of Wilson's preparedness possible, and when the Democratic Party met for its convention in St. Louis that same month, Woodrow Wilson was their candidate on the first ballot. The platform endorsed his Pan-American policy, his tariff law, his preparedness program, and it committed the Democratic Party to the idea of a league of nations.

Could a statesman ask for more wholehearted endorsement than that!

The Republicans had nominated Charles E. Hughes, a progressive who had been governor of New York and had won tremendous personal popularity in his work for reforms in government.

The Presidential campaign was a contest between two liberals, two men with reputations for high integrity and with tremendous audience appeal. The war and the postwar peace were the big issues, and very early the slogan began to circulate about Wilson: "He kept us out of the war!" Wilson was deeply distressed about it.

"I can't keep the country out of war," he said to Josephus Daniels. "They talk of me as though I were a god."

But there was no stopping the ardent Wilsonites who were stumping for him.

To heighten the excitement German submarines sank several ships off Nantucket in October and torpedoed a Red Cross liner. This brought the *Lusitania* debate back into the news and into the campaign.

Edith Wilson traveled with the President on most of his speaking tours, finding them far more strenuous and hectic than his western tour on behalf of preparedness. Once again the concluding speech was made in Madison Square Garden in New York City. The crowds in the streets around the Garden were so great that the Wilsons had to climb a fire escape and enter through a window. The moment Woodrow Wilson appeared on the platform an ovation burst forth that lasted for half an hour. "We want Wilson!" chanted the crowd. "Are you from Dixie?" blared the band.

Election Day was spent at Long Branch, New Jersey, and from there the Wilsons motored to Princeton so that he could vote.

"While my husband was in the old engine house voting," Mrs. Wilson wrote in her *Memoir,* "I sat in the car laughing with the boys who had pushed and jostled good-naturedly to get a glimpse of the President. When he came out they cheered him again. That was as near as I ever came to voting at the polls for a Presidential candidate."

Her good humor and charm had sustained him through a strenuous and taxing campaign, and now it was to sustain him through defeat or victory at the polls.

They returned to Long Branch where they settled down with Dr. Grayson, Frank Sayre, Margaret, and one or two others to await the results. In the evening, when polls began to close and tension began to gather, Edith Wilson suggested a game of Twenty Questions, and she succeeded in creating a little hilarity for a while. But the later the evening grew, the darker the election results began to look, and there was no more diversion; only grim restrained waiting. The totals on the tally sheets grew closer and closer and the face of the candidate grew taut as he set himself to accept the will of the people with dignity.

The phone rang around ten in the evening with a message from someone in New York saying that *The New York Times* building had flashed a signal indicating Hughes's victory.

"Impossible!" declared Margaret. "In the West they are still at the polls."

"Call Mr. Tumulty at headquarters," someone suggested.

Joe Tumulty explained that the tally count was far from final, but he was in a slough of despond. Due to the time difference between the East and the West the final results would probably not be known until late tomorrow. President Wilson decided that he would go to bed and try to sleep.

"I will not send Mr. Hughes a telegram of congratulations tonight, for things are not settled," he said. Even now his deepest thoughts were not for himself but for the nation. "There now seems little hope that we shall not be drawn into the war, though I have done everything I can to keep us out; but my defeat will be taken by Germany as a repudiation of my policy. Many of our own people will so construe it, and will try to force war upon the next administration."

Hughes would not commit himself either. The score was too close for comfort.

President Wilson said good night to everyone and withdrew, and as soon as he was out of the room others gave vent to their rage, particularly Margaret. She felt that the American people had betrayed her father and all he had done for them. Didn't they even remember the Federal Reserve System? Look at the friendship he was building with South America, the careful course he was steering with Mexico! What about the League of Nations! And the Sussex Pledge that he had wrung from Germany!

Most of them sat up and waited, and around four

in the morning the returns began to improve slightly, but Edith would not allow anyone to awaken the President.

The improvement was uncomfortably slight, and everyone in Wilson's circle lived in gloomy doubt from the closing of the polls on Tuesday until Thursday morning, when the Wilson family began to get ready to leave New Jersey.

Just then Dr. Grayson hurried in to say that he had heard California was safe. If this was so, then President Wilson was re-elected. *If* it was so! Everyone's mood began to change. There were even a few smiles.

In the afternoon President and Mrs. Wilson went aboard the *Mayflower,* still uncertain but at least hopeful, and sailed up the coast and up the Hudson to Rhinecliff, where their private train was to take them to Williamstown, Massachusetts, for a visit with Frank and Jessie Sayre and their children.

If they were hopeful, the cheering crowds that were waiting for them wherever they appeared were certainly convinced. By the time they reached Rhinecliff, about nine in the morning on Friday, a Democratic victory was a certainty. Their train was filled with flowers.

A few hours ago Woodrow and Edith Wilson had not known where their next home would be. But they knew now. After a visit with the Sayres, they returned to the White House.

The final tally, completed two weeks after Election Day, showed that Wilson had won over Hughes in the popular vote by little more than half a million votes and in the Electoral College by only twenty-three votes. Happily, the Democratic Party had resumed control in both houses, and so the re-elected President could hope for teamwork there.

In spite of the work that had accumulated on his desk, in spite of the fact that he was exhausted and plagued by neuritis and indigestion as a result of the national campaign, Woodrow Wilson could experience a sense of happiness in having been permitted to continue the task to which he felt so deeply called: the creation of a world organization to keep the peace. Realizing that the United States was being drawn closer and closer to entering the war in Europe, he considered it more imperative than ever to achieve peace. On December 18, 1916, he sent a message to all the belligerent governments, requesting them to state their "views as to the terms upon which the war might be concluded and the arrangements which would be deemed satisfactory as a guaranty against its renewal or the kindling of any similar conflict in the future . . ."

The idea of a League of Nations, in the face of the increasing war threat, and the rising emotions in the United States, was still one of the most fiercely debated subjects of the day. Many who had supported it a few months earlier began to reverse themselves.

Teddy Roosevelt, by now an excited saber rattler, began to denounce the idea he had once supported. Senator Lodge was opposed to a League. So were Senators William E. Borah of Idaho and Robert La Follette of Wisconsin—all men of tremendous influence!

A League would mean entangling alliances, they argued, and Jefferson had warned against this. It would mean an end of the Monroe Doctrine!

Wilson very soon called them "a little group of willful men." He arrived at momentous decisions slowly, but once a decision was made and he knew where he stood he became a dynamo to carry it through. The vision that he had of a world order must be made as visible and as clear to others as it was to himself.

He appeared before the United States Senate on the twenty-second of January, 1917, to tell them of the result of his peace query to the belligerents.

"The Central Powers united in a reply which stated merely that they were ready to meet their antagonists in conference to discuss terms of peace. The Entente Powers [Allies] have replied much more definitely and have stated, in general terms, indeed, but with sufficient definiteness to imply details, the arrangements, guarantees, and acts of reparation which they deem to be indispensable conditions of a satisfactory settlement. We are that much nearer a definite discussion of the peace which shall end the present war. We are that much nearer the discussion of the international concert which must thereafter hold the world at peace."

He made a stirring plea for the American people to provide the leadership in "that great enterprise." The New World must join with the Old in a "covenant of co-operative peace" or it would never be a success. And this "co-operative peace" must be just and without rancor. It "must be a peace without victory."

Peace without victory! The phrase stirred emotions in the Senate Chamber and everywhere in the world. The speech won him the respect and support of thousands upon thousands of Americans.

But soon after Woodrow Wilson's great speech for world peace, Joe Tumulty hurried into the President's office, white and shaken, and handed him an Associated Press bulletin. Wilson's face turned gray as he read that the Kaiser had already given secret orders to wage unrestricted submarine warfare upon all ships.

"This means war," Wilson said to his secretary. "The break that we have tried so hard to prevent now seems inevitable."

He sent first for his Secretary of State, and together they received the German Ambassador.

"My government could do nothing else," said the Ambassador.

"You must know that it cannot be accepted," replied Secretary Lansing.

After a few more comments, the Ambassador withdrew.

The release that had so shocked the President was also shocking the American people as headlines blazoned the news. Excitement was mounting as the sense of outrage deepened, and public opinion was spiraling upward into a will for war.

After a meeting with his Cabinet, President Wilson notified Germany that diplomatic relations were at an end, and the next day he addressed both Houses of Congress, telling them what they already knew: that Germany had violated her Sussex Pledge. The American Ambassador would be withdrawn from Berlin, and the German Ambassador had been handed his passport.

A short while later President Wilson asked Congress for authority to arm merchant ships.

In his Inaugural Address in March President Wilson spoke frankly of the grave situation to a solemn-faced audience.

"Peace cannot securely or justly rest upon an armed balance of power," he told them. Seas must be made equally free and safe for the use of all peoples. National armaments must be limited. "It is imperative that we should stand together. . . . United alike in the conception of our duty, and in the high resolve to perform it in the face of all men, let us dedicate ourselves to the great task to which we must now set our hand. For myself I beg your tolerance, your countenance, and your united aid . . ."

Thereupon he took the oath of office once more.

Immediately after the inauguration came news of the sinking of the S.S. *Algonquin,* then the *City of Memphis, Illinois,* and the *Vigilancia.* Out of Russia came news of revolt, of the abdication of the Czar replaced by a provisional government, which declared for civil liberties for the people and self-determination for such states as Finland, Poland, and Estonia.

Depressed by what he knew must be faced, yet steeling himself to face it, President Wilson called his Cabinet into session on the twentieth of March. Their faces were grim as they sat along either side of the polished wood table.

He reviewed for them everything he had done to prevent America's entry into the war.

"I should like to hear your views, gentlemen," he concluded.

The entire Cabinet had reached the same point in their thinking as the President.

"We are at war," said the Postmaster General.

"I have reluctantly made up my mind that action must be taken. We are at war," said the Secretary of Labor. "Congress should be called to declare that it exists."

The President turned to Secretary of the Navy Daniels.

"In view of Germany's broken promise to cease sinking American ships, I see no course except to declare war," said Mr. Daniels, and his face looked years older than it had a few hours before.

President Wilson immediately announced a special session of Congress for the second of April.

When he returned to the White House, it was to devote every ounce of his training and ability to writing a message for Congress whose every phrase was a needle, with one eye and a single point. His workday always began at six in the morning and lasted until midnight. Edith allowed no one to disturb him. They took luncheon alone. His only recreation was an occasional brief ride with Edith in the park. He slept very little at night.

He drafted this history-making message first in shorthand, then he rewrote it in a mixture of shorthand and longhand. Finally, he sat down at the typewriter himself to make the final copy.

On the evening of April 2, 1917, President and Mrs. Wilson, Dr. Grayson, and Mr. Tumulty drove to the Capitol through streets lined with crowds. In the Capitol the President left his companions and went to his own special room, where he could be alone except for a Secret Service man.

Woodrow Wilson, who had once peered through the palings in his father's churchyard at sick and starving prisoners of war, who had as an adolescent been shocked at the devastation wrought by Sherman's army in Columbia, must now ask Congress to repeat these tragedies.

He glanced at himself in a mirror and discovered that his own face was distorted with grief and worry.

He could not appear thus on such an occasion! With his right hand he smoothed out his face and set his jaw into place. Ready to play his role he walked toward the door of the meeting chamber. He heard the sound of a gavel and the Speaker's voice: "Gentlemen, the President of the United States!"

The door opened and he stepped into a packed room. Every member of the government, the Supreme Court, the Cabinet, diplomats were present. They rose to their feet and applauded.

When he took his place on the rostrum and laid the text of his message on the lectern before him, the room fell silent. His self-control, his dignity were splendid. He was every inch a President.

"I have called the Congress into extraordinary session because there are serious, very serious, choices of policy to be made, and made immediately, which it was neither right nor constitutionally permissible that I should assume the responsibility of making."

He reported to them the most recent events that had made this session necessary.

"With a profound sense of the solemn and even tragical character of the step I am taking and of the grave responsibilities which it involves, but in unhesitating obedience to what I deem my constitutional duty, I advise that the Congress declare the recent course of the Imperial German Government to be in fact nothing less than war against the government and people of the United States; that it formally accept the status of belligerent which has thus been thrust upon it . . .

"Our object now, as then, is to vindicate the principles of peace and justice in the life of the world. . . .

"The world must be made safe for democracy. Its peace must be planted upon the tested foundations of political liberty. We have no selfish ends to serve. We desire no conquest, no dominion. We seek no indemnities for ourselves, no material compensation for the sacrifices we shall freely make. We are but one of the champions of the rights of mankind. We shall be satisfied when those rights have been made as secure as the faith and the freedom of nations can make them. . . .

"To such a task we can dedicate our lives and our fortunes, everything that we are and everything that we have, with the pride of those who know that the day has come when America is privileged to spend her blood and her might for the principles that gave her birth and happiness and the peace which she has treasured. God helping her, she can do no other."

A breathless silence followed his last words. Many were openly weeping. Then a burst of cheers and deafening applause. Partisan politics were forgotten. They were united.

Joe Tumulty was at the President's side when they left the hall and walked into the Cabinet room.

"Our course from this time on is clear," the President said, and he spoke for several minutes, half to his secretary, half to himself, about the war that would have to be waged, when suddenly the whole ordeal overwhelmed him. He sank into a chair, laid his head on the table, and sobbed.

15. A War Is Won

THE frightful decision that Wilson had struggled so long and so earnestly to prevent was made, and as soon as Congress had declared war he became the dynamo of the war effort, rising to new and superb heights as Chief Executive of the nation. Carried along with him to these heights were such men as Secretary of the Navy Josephus Daniels; Secretary of the Treasury William G. McAdoo; Secretary of War Newton D. Baker, whom Wilson had appointed just a year before; Joseph P. Tumulty, his personal secretary; Rear Admiral Cary T. Grayson, his physician; Colonel Edward M. House, who has been called by Professor Link the "man closest to the throne."

Party lines and differences were forgotten as prominent statesmen and businessmen hastened to volunteer their services. Princeton alumnus Cleveland H. Dodge came to the White House to help create a Red Cross War Council. Former President William Howard Taft was chairman of the Red Cross Executive Committee. Herbert Hoover had been in London for the Commission for Relief in Belgium, succeeding to an amazing extent in getting food through the blockade. President Wilson appointed Mr. Hoover the United States Food Administrator.

"The President made appointments irrespective of political faiths," Herbert Hoover wrote years later. "No more splendid men could have been found than Bernard M. Baruch, who directed the War Industries Board; Secretary of the Treasury W. G. McAdoo, who was also Railway Administrator; Harry A. Garfield, who directed the Fuel Administration; Charles M. Schwab, who directed ship construction; Edward N. Hurley, who managed the overseas shipping; and Vance M. McCormick, who directed the controls over imports, exports and blockade matters."

Former Republican Senator Elihu Root, already a member of the Court of Arbitration at The Hague and an advocate of the League of Nations, headed a commission which President Wilson sent to Russia "to convey to the Russian Government the friendship and good will of this nation . . . [and] with the duty of finding the most efficient means of cooperation . . . in the prosecution of the war."

William Jennings Bryan, immediately after the declaration of war, sent a telegram to the President:

"Please enroll me as a private whenever I am needed. . . . I shall through the Red Cross contribute to the comfort of soldiers in the hospitals and through the YMCA. . . ."

The President's son-in-law Francis B. Sayre went overseas for the YMCA, and his daughter Margaret traveled about the United States, singing for the men in camps.

The whole economy had to be geared to the task of the war, and many democratic rights and privileges—as dear to Woodrow Wilson as to anyone—had to be set aside. One offensive necessity was censorship, which President Wilson had to declare "necessary to the public safety," but cooperation from the news services was as wholeheartedly given as from every other group, and prominent newsmen joined his staff. Ray Stannard Baker became Wilson's public relations adviser and eventually his official biographer. George Creel became chairman of the Commission of War Information, and Marvin H. McIntyre was Special Assistant to the Secretary of the Navy. McIntyre eventually became President Franklin D. Roosevelt's secretary.

One of the gravest steps that President Wilson had to take was the Military Conscription Law. Conscription was an old European evil that thousands of refugees had come to America to escape, and Wilson at first found the idea repulsive. But he soon announced that conscription would be necessary.

Wilson had already witnessed the depth of a religious pacifist's convictions in men like Bryan and the Quaker Hoover, and conscientious objectors of various religious faiths were given noncombatant duty, although those who resisted the draft were sent to prison. Wilson felt sympathy for any man with the courage of his own convictions, and he was not alone in that feeling.

"I am a pacifist," declared Newton D. Baker, Secretary of War. "I am a pacifist in my hope; I am a pacifist in my prayers; I am a pacifist in my belief that God made man for better things than that civilization should always be under the blight of this increasingly deadly destruction which war leaves us."

A permanent peace after the war was a living dream in many hearts. Woodrow Wilson and Colonel House had already written a first draft of a constitution for a League of Nations.

Meanwhile the war program was expensive, and even though Wilson was a scrupulous pay-as-you-go Scot he knew that enough money could not be raised by taxation for so staggering a task. To meet the need the Treasury Department issued Liberty Loan Bonds in small denominations so that people with modest incomes could buy them. The response was tremendous.

"Americans are investing at the rate of nearly twenty million dollars an hour!" Wilson told Edith shortly after the First Liberty Loan Drive was launched, and he was radiant when he said it. The splendid cooperation was not merely at the top. It was nationwide.

Edith Wilson gave every spare minute to Red Cross and other war work. Late at night the whir of her sewing machine could be heard. She grew impatient with sturdy young men who complained of long hours. Her husband rose at five in the morning, was at his desk by six, and was not through until midnight. She had to be on the alert to see that he took some recreation, a drive, a walk in the White House gardens, a round of golf.

He was as impatient as she when he heard complaints about what people *thought* were food shortages. They had never lived on soup made from cowpeas nor used cut plug tobacco for currency. They weren't starving to death as were people in countries occupied by the Central Powers.

A war always means mobilization of every resource, economizing, and belt-tightening. President Wilson had asked Herbert Hoover "to work towards saving food and eliminating waste," and within a few months America had to accept "meatless days," and "sweetless days." Everyone who owned any land was asked to grow and preserve his own vegetables. America was "Hooverizing" to win the war. The government assigned places in public parks for vegetable gardens to those who did not own land. Wartime gardens began to appear everywhere. The stretch of land along the Potomac in the national capital where Japanese cherry trees now bloom was filled with vegetable gardens during World War I. People with full-time office jobs worked in them early in the morning and in the evening.

The war in Europe at the time that the United States became an associate of the Allies was still at a stalemate. The Allied countries were reaching the exhaustion of both men and supplies; the Germans were holding a long line of defense known as the Hindenburg Line that the British and French armies were unable to break through; submarines were destroying thousands of tons of shipping.

General Pershing was given command of the American Expeditionary Forces, and Admiral William S. Sims was in command of naval forces. Weeks passed while American troops were being trained and equipped, and Allied morale in Europe sank lower. The first United States troops sailed for Europe in June, 1917. They were convoyed, to be sure, but crossing thousands of miles of submarine-infested waters. The whole nation lived through twelve days of tense waiting until at last the wireless message came that the entire group had arrived safely.

During the eighteen months that the United States was at war two million men were shipped overseas, and not one transport was ever sunk by a U-boat.

President Wilson, who felt such a deep personal responsibility for the young men whom he was sending into combat, was at least spared that additional anguish.

"No man has ever had deeper or graver responsibilities," said Colonel House, "and no one has met them with more patience, courage, and wisdom."

In the late autumn of 1917 Wilson asked his friend House to go to Europe as head of an American War Mission to coordinate all Allied efforts. A similar British Mission had come to the United States. While he was abroad Colonel House had ample opportunity to study at close range, often at private dinner parties, the personalities and thinking of British Prime Minister David Lloyd George and French Premier Georges Clemenceau, priceless information for Woodrow Wilson when he finally met with them himself.

As 1917 drew to a close the war situation in Europe grew darker and more sinister for the Allies. The provisional government in Russia, friendly to the Allies, lasted less than eight months. A Bolshevik regime, militant and ruthless, seized power and set up a government headed by Lenin and Trotsky. The new government began peace negotiations with the Central Powers in November.

A man did not need to be a military expert to know what that would mean. Germany no longer had to fight on her Eastern Front. She could withdraw thousands of troops and throw them at the British, French, and Americans on the Western Front.

And the Italian front was collapsing!

"With the apparent total collapse of Russia and the recent success of the Central Powers in Italy, German morale is undoubtedly much improved and the probability of a serious offensive against the Western Front is greatly increased. . . . In view of these conditions it is of the utmost importance to the Allied cause that we move swiftly . . ." General Pershing wired to Secretary Baker.

"The entire situation is critical," House cabled to Wilson.

President Wilson did "move swiftly." Only a small portion of the ultimate two million soldiers to go abroad had been sent so far. The number must be stepped up. One bottleneck holding up both men and materials was poor transportation service in the United States. President Wilson issued a proclamation placing the railroads under government operation for the duration of the war. Taking a hard look at the coal situation he declared "heatless days" to conserve fuel. When a labor union threatened to slow down activity in the shipyards, the President treated it to a needle-pointed message:

"Will you cooperate or will you obstruct?"

The administration was doing its utmost to maintain proper working conditions and fair wages, and most labor leaders realized it.

There was a gross lack of unity among the Allies in their planning and their aims, and they could not be persuaded to agree. Wilson seized this problem by the horns. Since the Allies could not agree on aims, America must take the initiative in defining them, and he was America's voice.

After long secluded hours at his desk, writing, rewriting, correcting, typing, he delivered on January 8, 1918, his history-shaping speech on "The Fourteen Points."

"We entered this war because violations of right had occurred which touched us to the quick and made the life of our own people impossible unless they were corrected and the world secured once for all against their recurrence. . . . for our own part we see very clearly that unless justice be done to others it will not be done to us."

There must be no secret agreements, he said. "Open covenants of peace, openly arrived at," freedom of the seas in peace and in war, removal of trade barriers, reduction of armaments, impartial adjustment of colonial claims, evacuation of invaded territories, independence for Poland, these were covered in his first thirteen points. The fourteenth point gave all the others sticking power:

"A general association of nations must be formed under specific covenants for the purpose of affording mutual guarantees of political independence and territorial integrity to great and small states alike. . . .

"We stand together until the end."

Copies of Woodrow Wilson's speech on the Fourteen Points went round the world on the press wires. It raised hopes in millions of hearts and gave new courage to many statesmen in other lands.

But not all statesmen were in favor of the Fourteen Points, and many of the military leaders wanted Germany crushed, humiliated, punished for her war guilt. They wanted conquering armies to march across Germany; Berlin must be burned to the ground.

The man who had written the Fourteen Points had also coined the phrase, "Peace without victory." He had meant what he said, and before very much longer the world would realize it.

Meanwhile the war grew worse. More and more men were sent overseas. Casualty lists appeared daily in the newspapers. The pinches grew more severe.

In the spring of 1918 Germany launched a fierce offensive against the Western Front, advancing as far as forty miles in some places. To stop the advance and plan a counteradvance General Ferdinand Foch was made Commander in Chief of the Allied forces. In May came another German attack with further advances into France. In the heat and mud of late July the Second Battle of the Marne raged, and the Allies, strengthened by thousands of fresh troops from America, began to drive the Germans back. Early in August the tide of war at last turned. The Allies continued to gain advances in the battles of Amiens, the Somme, and Arras, and American forces won a victory at St.

Mihiel in September. After that came the battles of the Argonne and Ypres which dealt further weakening blows upon German lines.

Among starved and war-weary Germans morale was sinking and revolt was growing against their military regime. Bulgaria collapsed in October, and Austria-Hungary was teetering on the brink of collapse.

The German Government sent a message to President Wilson that it was ready to negotiate peace based on the Fourteen Points. The offer was foxy, meant to avoid surrender and the humiliation of being crushed militarily. But in America the hue and cry was for destroying Germany. Wilson wanted peace without victory; he did not want bloody vengeance; but he was not fooled by the German message. Men were still fighting in the trenches; U-boats were still sinking ships. Wilson felt that Germany was stalling for time to reorganize her forces. If the United States must deal with "the military masters" of Germany, Wilson replied, then surrender could be the only reply.

The German people themselves responded. Their smoldering revolution burst its bonds, mutiny broke out in the navy, spreading to the rest of the country. The Kaiser's abdication was forced, and a republic proclaimed. This government was the nearest to representative rule that the German people could hope for in their then paralyzed state of poverty, despair, and defeat.

But the air was still full of the hysterical demands for vengeance, and so were the Allied commands. It is to President Wilson's eternal glory that he was able to prevent the overrunning of Germany with a "Sherman March." If the Allies would not negotiate for peace, then the United States would negotiate separately. The United States was not an Ally by any treaty arrangement at all, they must remember; she was an *associate*. The Allies capitulated.

At home the first public reaction was deeply resentful against Wilson, and the American people were about to go to the polls to elect a new House of Representatives and a third of the Senate. Republican Party campaigners played up the President's "weakness." Teddy Roosevelt wanted "peace by the hammering guns and not chat about peace . . ."

Without a supporting Congress, particularly the Senate which must ratify any treaties or international commitments, President Wilson's role of world statesman would be meaningless.

All during the war effort he had remained aloof from politics, and he would have preferred to do so in this election. But when he realized how much confused thinking was being created, he decided to go directly to the people once more. He made a public appeal for a Democratic Congress.

"If you have approved of my leadership and wish me to continue to be your unembarrassed spokesman in affairs at home and abroad, I earnestly beg that you will express yourselves unmistakably to that effect by returning a Democratic majority to both the Senate and the House of Representatives."

The effect was anything but good. What about Republicans who have supported you in the war program? demanded the opposition.

Thoughtful Republicans like Herbert Hoover, who were willing to understand the true intent of Wilson's appeal, and its reasonableness, gave him their public endorsement.

"I did so because I believed that the President's hand in the Treaty negotiations would be greatly weakened if the election went against him," said Mr. Hoover.

But partisan reaction and a rising tide of isolationism, combined with votes of those who wanted war vengeance, turned the elections against the Democratic Party in so many states that it lost control of both Houses. Wilson refused to admit discouragement, but he and Edith were depressed by the news, nonetheless.

While the election returns were coming in, arrangements were being made for a meeting between the Allied military command and a German armistice commission. General Foch received them in his private railway coach in Compiègne Forest on the seventh of November. General Foch presented the conditions for an armistice, a staying of arms, so that a peace treaty could be drawn up by the various governments. The principal requirements were that Germany must withdraw her troops from all occupied territory, and she must surrender a long inventory of trucks, freight cars, submarines, and warships. The commission then sent the terms home to its foreign office for approval or rejection. Hostilities could not cease until an agreement was reached.

Meanwhile President Wilson was conferring with Herbert Hoover and Secretary Lansing about plans for sending American relief to the starving millions of Europe.

"The idea of America is to serve humanity."

General Foch had scarcely met with the commission in Compiègne Forest when the United Press released a news announcement that an armistice had been signed. The country went wild with cheering crowds, whistles, sirens. Offices and factories closed, schools sent children home, and people rushed out into the streets laughing, crying, shouting, dancing, with delirious relief.

A dense crowd gathered around the White House, and a band began to play. They shouted for a sight of their President.

Edith hurried to his study and begged him to show himself on the portico and wave to the crowd.

He shook his head. "There is no armistice," he told her. The guns were still booming; men were still dying.

Gradually the hilarity died down as people realized that the report had been false.

On Sunday the President and Mrs. Wilson went to

church in the morning and had luncheon by themselves. They spent the afternoon and evening decoding and answering messages, and the task helped them through the tense waiting.

At three o'clock on Monday morning, November 11, 1918, President Wilson received the news for which he had been waiting so long: the Armistice was a fact. It had just been signed. The guns were at last silent. The killing had ceased.

"My Fellow Countrymen," said his Presidential announcement. "The armistice was signed this morning. Everything for which America fought has been accomplished. It will now be our fortunate duty to assist by example, by sober, friendly counsel and by material aid in the establishment of just democracy throughout the world. Woodrow Wilson."

16. A Peace Is Lost

A JUST democracy throughout the world was possible only through a league of nations to enforce both peace and justice. To this great purpose Woodrow Wilson was dedicated. Everyone who knew Wilson knew this, and the whole world knew Wilson. He was its leading statesman.

Through the pressing multitude of demobilization problems and all the domestic issues before Congress, President Wilson worked on the planning for the Peace Conference to be held in Paris. A commission would go from the United States, and he must choose the men as well as their leader. The other countries attending—Great Britain, France, Italy, Japan, Greece, Poland, etc.—would send their prime ministers rather than king or president, but in the United States the President is both chief executive and chief diplomat. After very careful deliberation, in spite of objections from high and low, Wilson decided to go himself as leader of the commission.

But the President must never leave the United

States! cried the objectors. Colonel House, already in Europe helping to coordinate arrangements for the Conference, cabled home: "Clemenceau has just told me that he hopes you will not sit in the Congress because no head of a state should sit there. The same feeling prevails in England."

Wilson knew that many motives went into those appeals. He was a liberal with the interest of the common people frankly at heart. "Let the people come forward," he had said at his first inauguration as President. His bold forthrightness, his desire for "open covenants openly arrived at," was another trait that could prove embarrassing to Old World diplomats accustomed to dealing and dickering in secret. He was already being besieged by petitions from favor-seeking national groups who hoped to grab something for themselves from the realignments. What must not the big nations have in mind! There were German colonies to be disposed of. There were choice areas on the Continent to be seized. Great Britain did not really approve freedom of the seas. And the air was filled with bitterness and hatred and passion for revenge.

An entire ship was necessary to transport the personnel of the American Peace Commission. The President and Mrs. Wilson, Secretary of State and Mrs. Lansing, Dr. Grayson, personal attendants, secretaries, Secret Service men, guards, totaling more than a thousand persons, were aboard the *George Washington* when she sailed on December 4, 1918.

The voyage took ten days, and even though President Wilson accomplished a great deal of work en route the sea air, the quiet, the smooth crossing, rested and restored him for the ordeal ahead.

The restful atmosphere vanished as the ship approached the harbor of Brest. French destroyers escorted the *George Washington* in. President and Mrs. Wilson and their immediate party stood on deck and received a host of officials who boarded the ship to greet them. Among them were General Pershing and Admiral Sims.

The harbor and shores were dense with hysterically happy people waiting to catch a glimpse of "Wilson the Just." Brest is in Brittany, and the people had dressed in their bright and gay traditional costumes.

"Vive! Vive!" they shouted as they waved colored scarves. "Hail! Hail!"

The personal train of the President of France waited to take them to Paris and a long red carpet had been laid through the railway station approaching it. Every mile of the way to Paris there were cheering throngs to welcome the representative of the nation that had sent the troops to turn the tide of war, the author of the Fourteen Points, the statesman who would exert every moral force to bring justice to small nations and depressed groups.

They fairly worshiped him, like a god who could grant their every wish, and this worried Wilson. He knew they expected many things that would be humanly impossible to accomplish. While his heart nearly burst with the love they bestowed upon him it ached at the disappointments they would have to face.

In Paris the President and Mrs. Wilson were received by the President of France, Raymond Poincaré, and Madame Poincaré, the French Cabinet, and the American Ambassador. There followed a round of official banquets, teas, receptions.

Some of this diplomacy was necessary, but President Wilson knew there was a certain amount of delaying going on, and he began to grow impatient. Parties were not what he had come for, and he had left a busy desk at home to which he must return within a reasonable length of time.

But it was apparent that the Conference would not be convened for another month, and so in the meantime Woodrow and Edith Wilson made official trips to England and Italy. The same excited, hopeful crowds waited to cheer them everywhere. And they visited hospitals full of wounded soldiers wherever they went. At an American hospital in Neuilly, France, he and Edith spent hours, visiting at every bedside, trying to hide their shock and keep their eyes dry. When a doctor escorted them into a "facial ward" Edith was afraid she would faint: "some with their entire noses blown away, some totally blind, others with chins and half their faces gone."

At last on January 18, 1919, the opening session of the Peace Conference came to order around a huge horseshoe-shaped table in the Salle de la Paix (Hall of Peace) in the Ministry of Foreign Affairs on the Quai d'Orsay in Paris, the famous street along the left bank of the Seine River. There were delegates representing twenty-seven nations.

For the sake of efficiency it had been decided to have an executive group, a Council of Ten, that would meet every day; and eventually the ten became four, the "Big Four": Wilson, Clemenceau, who was the permanent chairman, Lloyd George, and Orlando.

Woodrow Wilson already knew their personalities.

Georges Clemenceau, Premier of France, was known as "The Tiger." He was a heavy-set man with a shaggy mustache and a fiery disposition. He was forthright in his manner with a singleness of purpose, to make France secure from future attacks across the Rhine. He could be fierce or gentle; he could use his claws or hide them. He was willing to try Wilson's League of Nations, but being a practical Frenchman he did not hope for very much.

David Lloyd George, Prime Minister of Great Britain, short, white-haired, liberal, witty, and charming, a colorful Welshman, was the changeable type. He would take a stand on an issue and then cunningly reverse himself. As far as Wilson could see Lloyd George had come to seize any advantage he could for England, but he did not have Wilson's long-range goals in mind. How different Gladstone would have been!

Vittorio Orlando, Premier of Italy, was another short man, white-haired, mustachioed, full of temperament. He had come to obtain what he could for Italy, but he lacked political finesse.

In the opinion of Dr. Grayson who saw a great deal of the "Big Four" at close range, "none of them possessed the prophetic qualities of Mr. Wilson who looked beyond the immediate results of the Peace Conference to the far-off future of Europe and the world."

When Dr. Grayson, who knew the President's health better than anyone, tried to counsel Wilson against overworking—he had given up all recreation and even worked on Sunday—Wilson replied, "The world is on fire." Huge armies had not yet been demobilized but stood poised and waiting to go back into combat.

There were great pressures on the Conference to maintain the existing armies, particularly in France, and there were pressures for boundary changes, for making Germany's colonies spoils of war, for making Germany pay war damages and reparations, for punishing Germany with a severe and vengeful treaty.

To Woodrow Wilson, who was dedicated to disarmament, to just boundaries wherever possible, and to holding hate and greed in check, the most important issue was the League of Nations. He made that his first aim and his first achievement.

He opened the second general session on January 25 with a stirring speech urging that a League covenant be made an inseparable part of the Peace Treaty. He made a profound impression, and to his great joy a resolution was passed favoring the idea and a special commission was appointed to draft the covenant. Colonel House, who had worked with the President months ago in drafting a preliminary version, was a member of this commission.

Any group under Mr. Wilson's direction worked hard. The news correspondent, Ray Stannard Baker, called it "the hardest-driven commission in Paris." It had a tentative draft of the Covenant—Section I of the Treaty—ready for the third session on the fourteenth of February. The League it proposed was to have a Secretariat at Geneva, and an executive Council of the five great powers with four others elected by the Body of Delegates. All member nations would be represented in the Body of Delegates. The purpose of the League would be "to promote international cooperation and to secure international peace and security . . . by the prescription of open, just and honorable relations between nations . . ." It was to strive for disarmament, for improved labor conditions and better health, and its greatest motive was to prevent armed conflict.

Edith Wilson and Dr. Grayson were given special permission to attend the Conference and hear the President's address. This hour was surely the zenith of his career, the presentation of his dream to the assembled nations.

"It was a great moment in history," Edith wrote,

"as he stood there—slender, calm, and powerful in his argument—I seemed to see the people of all depressed countries—men, women and little children—crowding round and waiting upon his words."

When he had finished the delegates received their ballots. The tally showed that the Covenant of the League of Nations was approved as Section I of the Peace Treaty!

The audience arose cheering and applauding and hurried to the front of the room to clasp Wilson's hand.

As they drove back to their hotel, Edith asked the President, "Are you weary?"

He replied: "Yes, I suppose I am, but how little one man means when such vital things are at stake. . . . It will be sweet to go home, even for a few days, with the feeling that I have kept the faith with the people, particularly with these boys, God bless them."

That same night they took a train to the coast and went aboard the *George Washington* bound for America. The President had to be home for the final sessions of Congress before it adjourned. He must consider every piece of legislation that had been enacted. Colonel House remained in Paris to act in the President's stead until he could return.

The whole history-making affair had been covered by the newspapers, and when the President and Mrs. Wilson docked in Boston they were greeted by Governor and Mrs. Calvin Coolidge and heart-warming crowds. They hurried to Washington, where the President met immediately with the Foreign Relations Committees of both Houses. He gave them a detailed account and copies of the drafted Covenant, urging them to do their utmost for it. He was acutely aware of the increasing isolationism in America, and he asked Senator Lodge,

"Do you think it will go through the Senate?"

Senator Lodge, chairman of the Senate Foreign Relations Committee, replied, "If the Foreign Relations Committee approves it, I feel there is no doubt of ratification."

President Wilson assumed from that statement that Lodge was going to support the League of Nations, but the comment had been cunningly worded.

Wilson arrived back in Paris the middle of March to be greeted by the comment, "Your League is dead."

The whole situation had deteriorated in his absence. Enemies of the League had gleefully waited for him to leave, and they had busily worked to discredit the League and have it omitted from the Peace Treaty.

Wilson was shocked and angry; he was most angry with Colonel House.

"House has given away everything I had won before we left Paris," he told Edith that evening. "He has compromised on every side."

House was simply not an uncompromising Scot, and he had been no match for the cunning of European politicians bent on war spoils and reparations. The intimacy between Wilson and House had been fading, and this episode brought it to an end.

Edith Wilson had long ago developed a distrust of Colonel House, and on one occasion she had said to her husband: "It seems to me that it is impossible for two persons always to think alike, and while I like Colonel House immensely, I find him absolutely colourless and a 'yes, yes' man."

The President had not agreed with her then, and since Edith knew how valuable House was to him she held her peace and made it a point to be gracious.

Others had shared her opinion of House, and now House had revealed himself to be more of a "yes, yes" man than the President had ever realized.

Woodrow Wilson took hold of the situation in Paris immediately. The League Covenant must be saved, otherwise every American doughboy would be betrayed.

With the help of Ray Stannard Baker, the President issued a press release: "The President said today that the decision made at the Peace Conference at its plenary session, January 25, 1919, to the effect that the establishment of a League of Nations should be made an integral part of the Treaty of Peace, is of final force and that there is no basis whatever for the reports that a change in this decision was contemplated."

It caught his opponents off guard and cleared the air at once. He went on from there to hold a conference with Clemenceau and Lloyd George to work out an open and aboveboard basis for agreement in their thinking. He had had enough of Old World conniving!

The Conference moved ahead with new impetus, to make final revisions in the League Covenant, and Wilson gave particular attention to suggestions from William Howard Taft, Elihu Root, and Charles E. Hughes, realizing that their suggestions would make the Covenant more acceptable to a Republican-dominated Senate. It was Mr. Taft who suggested the additional phrase: "Nothing in this Covenant shall be deemed to affect the validity of international engagements, such as treaties of arbitration or regional understandings like the Monroe Doctrine . . ."

In the midst of completing the other treaty terms, Wilson was stricken with influenza, an epidemic then raging in both Europe and America. It kept him helpless in bed for three days and forced a tedious recovery upon him. But he still would not listen to his doctor. As soon as he was on his feet, however weak, gaunt, and haggard, he was back at work.

By the middle of April the Big Four were ready to publish the almost final results of their months of deliberation.

The terms of the document, soon to be known as the Versailles Treaty, fell far short of Woodrow Wilson's hopes. He had had to yield to compromises. Germany must assume "war guilt." The reparations payments to be demanded of her would prevent her from economic recovery for years to come. She must surrender a big portion of her merchant and fishing fleets, and her army and navy could be only token forces.

But at least he had succeeded in having German colonies placed under a mandate of the future League. The independence of such small nations as Austria, Czechoslovakia, and Poland was guaranteed. The Treaty did contain the Covenant of a League of Nations. Wilson saw in the Covenant the factor that would ease and soften and revise the other terms in future years as hatred and bitterness faded.

On the twenty-eighth of June, 1919, representatives of the Allied and German nations met in the Hall of Mirrors in Versailles Palace, about ten miles outside of Paris, to sign the treaty. In that same room in 1871, after the surrender of Paris to German troops in the Franco-Prussian War, William I was crowned Emperor of Germany, a bitter memory to the French. This day the defeat of William II, the Kaiser, was secure.

Cheering throngs were again waiting to cry, *"Vive* Wilson!" when the party emerged, and so it was all the way back to the ship and again in New York City where he was officially greeted by Governor Alfred E. Smith.

Woodrow Wilson was not taken in by the cheering. He had been kept informed by diplomatic and political grapevines and by the press of the protests developing in both England and the United States. There were protests that the punishment of Germany had not been severe enough, protests about the drawing of almost every boundary line on the Continent. In America the severest protests were against involvement in a League of Nations. Bitterness was increasing because the postwar economy was going into a recession. War production had ended, and thousands of demobilized men were coming home unable to find jobs.

Weeks before the Versailles meeting Senator Lodge had made a speech before the Senate against America's entrance into the League. America would have to "give up in part our sovereignty and independence and subject our own will to the will of other nations." The next step in his strategy was to present an anti-League resolution to the Senate which contained the signatures of thirty-seven senators.

Now that Woodrow Wilson was home with his finger on the domestic pulse, he realized that another fight would have to be waged if the United States was to participate in the League of Nations. He must once more move swiftly.

He made his formal presentation of the Treaty of Versailles to the United States Senate for its ratification on the tenth of July. He spoke of the good faith and sacrifice of the more than 300,000 men who had been killed or wounded; he reviewed the major problems of the Peace Conference. He appealed to their sense of right and justice for "a League of Nations to steady the counsels and maintain the peaceful understandings of the world . . ."

Senator Hiram W. Johnson of California, William

E. Borah of Idaho, and Robert La Follette of Wisconsin were the chief supporters of Senator Lodge in his opposition to the League Covenant being included in the Treaty. They unleashed propaganda, and they went on speaking tours. The whole country became embroiled in a deeply bitter controversy.

In conferences with his supporters in the Senate and in the Democratic Party, Woodrow Wilson saw that he must go once more directly to the American people, and he planned a speaking tour of the West where isolationist feelings were the most intense.

Dr. Grayson feared for the President's life if he attempted such an arduous task, and he hurried to Mr. Wilson's office.

"I know what you have come for," said the President. "I do not want to do anything foolhardy but the League of Nations is now in its crisis, and if it fails I hate to think what will happen to the world."

Woodrow Wilson had never been thinner; his neuritis bothered him; his left eyelid twitched occasionally; his digestion was poor; he had been suffering from severe headaches and attacks of asthma ever since his Paris ordeal.

Edith was desperately worried, and yet she knew she could not stop him from sacrificing himself.

The President's special train pulled out of Washington on the third of September. Accompanying the President were Mrs. Wilson, Dr. Grayson, Mr. Tumulty, their personal servants, and the usual guards.

For the next three weeks Wilson gave two and three speeches a day, and he traveled continually between engagements. Dr. Grayson and Edith watched as he expended himself.

Yet, when he was before an audience, particularly when he sensed that the audience was receiving his words well, his personality glowed; from somewhere within him came an amazing energy, his eyes shone, and his cheeks took on color. This was his mission! To this he had been called!

Ohio, Indiana, Missouri, Iowa, Nebraska, the Dakotas, Montana, Idaho, Washington, Oregon, California, Nevada, Utah, Colorado! In between speeches he shook hands with thousands, talked with newsmen and local leaders. He spoke in huge halls, in tents, from the rear platform of his train.

"This treaty is unique in the history of mankind," he told his listeners, "because the center of it is the redemption of weak nations. There never was a congress of nations before that considered the rights of those who could not enforce their rights."

And again, "If there is no league of nations, the military point of view will prevail in every instance, and peace will be brought into contempt."

Patiently he explained every detail. "In the midst of the treaty of peace is a Magna Charta, a great guarantee for labor. It provides that labor shall have the counsels of the world devoted to the discussion of its conditions and of its betterment."

His headaches and asthmatic attacks were growing more severe, his ability to sleep less and less.

When the train reached Pueblo, Colorado, he said to Edith, "This will have to be a short speech."

But before the audience his strength reappeared and he gave one of the most moving talks of the campaign.

That evening his headache was so severe that it almost blinded him, and shortly before midnight he called to Edith and admitted that he felt ill. She sent for Dr. Grayson, and they both stayed with the President through the night. He slept for only about two hours toward morning and awoke with the intention of speaking in Kansas.

Dr. Grayson shook his head. He recognized the symptoms of complete nervous breakdown. There could be no more speeches. The rest of the tour must be canceled.

The train carried him back to the nation's capital where he was hurried to the White House and to bed. The pains in his head were so severe that he could not concentrate on anything. For the next three days he rested completely and seemed to be recovering. He began to appear better, even to his doctor.

Edith got up frequently during every night to look at him. Around five in the morning on October second she found him resting comfortably and asleep, but when she returned to him at eight he was sitting on the edge of the bed, his left hand limp at his side.

"I have no feeling in that hand," he said. "Will you rub it?"

The side of his face was sagging as well, and she rushed to the phone to summon Dr. Grayson.

When she hurried back to the President, Grayson close upon her heels, she found Woodrow Wilson unconscious on the floor. They lifted him to the bed, and the doctor knew that he had suffered a paralytic stroke on the left side.

He was never physically well again. For the remaining months of his term of office Edith talked with government men for him and brought him only a minimum of problems. He recovered partially and was able to see one Cabinet member or Senator at a time, and soon he was even able to hold a Cabinet meeting. It did not help his recovery to know that Senator Lodge and the Republican Party were killing any chance of America's participation in the League of Nations.

To him the birth of the League of Nations was "the birth of the spirit of the times," a living thing. If America did not participate, he had already foretold, "there will soon be a breakup of the world that will be no mere war, but a cataclysm."

Quietly he listened to reports of the debate in the Senate, and on the nineteenth of March, 1920, he was told that the Senate had voted 49 to 35 against ratifying the Treaty of Versailles.

"I feel like going to bed and staying there," said Woodrow Wilson.

The Democratic Party held its Presidential Convention in California in June, and its platform promised ratification of the Treaty and the League of Nations. Very soon thereafter the candidates—Governor James M. Cox of Ohio for President and Franklin Delano Roosevelt of New York for Vice President—called upon President Wilson. They found him sitting in an easy chair on a portico of the White House, withered and wasted, wrapped in a warm shawl. He did not even notice their approach.

"Mr. President," said FDR, "we are going to be a million per cent with you, and your administration, and that means the League of Nations."

Wilson felt a twinge of the old fire in his heart. FDR was a man of boundless energy and ability.

"I am very grateful," he told his visitors.

He was far too ill to participate in the campaign himself, but he sent letters and messages to others, during the summer and fall, urging the acceptance of the League of Nations "to vindicate the country's honor." Toward the end of October, sitting in his wheel chair, he was able to receive a group of pro-League Republican leaders at the White House.

On Election Day, November 2, 1920, the Republican Senator from Ohio, Warren G. Harding, an isolationist, was elected to the Presidency by a big popular majority. Thus, the United States did not join the League of Nations.

But the year before, Woodrow Wilson had received

the Nobel Peace Prize—a tribute from the peoples of Europe.

Woodrow Wilson's physical condition improved sufficiently to permit him to participate in the Inauguration in March, although he stood painfully with the aid of a cane. He and Edith had moved from the White House to 2340 S Street in Washington, D.C., taking with them among their other possessions Wilson's bookcase, the one purchased with the first money he had ever earned. His library of eight thousand books would scarcely fit into it now.

They lived in S Street for nearly three years, receiving visitors, most of whom came to pay tribute to the great statesman. Woodrow Wilson made occasional public appearances, and his last public speech was on November 11, 1923, when he addressed the nation over the radio on "The High Significance of Armistice Day."

Wilson's eyesight began to fail, and on the last day of January, 1924, his physical condition grew suddenly worse. Margaret and Edith were with him late Sunday morning, February 3, 1924, when Woodrow Wilson drifted quietly into his final sleep.

The great peace warrior had fallen, but he had not dropped his torch. He had handed it on to a future President.

Bibliography

Principal Sources

Alsop, Em Bowles (Editor). *The Greatness of Woodrow Wilson.* New York: Rinehart & Company, Inc., 1956.
Compiled for the Woodrow Wilson Centennial Celebration Commission, this is a comprehensive collection of essays on Woodrow Wilson by eighteen prominent persons, with an introduction by former President Dwight D. Eisenhower.

Baker, Ray Stannard. *Woodrow Wilson, Life and Letters,* 8 volumes. Garden City, New York: Doubleday, Page & Company, 1927–1939. *Woodrow Wilson and World Settlement,* 2 volumes. Garden City, New York: Doubleday, Page & Company, 1922.
These ten volumes are the legacy of a brilliant scholar and personal friend of the late President Wilson, who enjoyed access to both his public and private papers. They comprise a basic resource for any study of Mr. Wilson's life.

Daniels, Jonathan. *The End of Innocence.* Philadelphia: J. B. Lippincott Company, 1954.
Written by the son of Mr. Wilson's Secretary of the Navy, this volume is a fine interpretation of the balance of personalities in Washington during the Wilson era, especially William Jennings Bryan, Colonel House, and other members of the Cabinet.

Daniels, Josephus. *The Wilson Era,* 2 volumes. Chapel Hill: The University of North Carolina Press, 1944, 1946.
Valuable recollections and evaluations by President Wilson's Secretary of the Navy.

Elliott, Margaret Axson. *My Aunt Louisa and Woodrow*

Wilson. Chapel Hill: The University of North Carolina Press, 1944.

Exclusive personal recollections of the young sister-in-law to whom Mr. Wilson was a foster father.

Grayson, Rear Admiral Cary T. *Woodrow Wilson, An Intimate Memoir*. New York: Holt, Rinehart and Winston, 1960.

As the title implies, the intimate memoir of President Wilson's personal physician while he was in the White House.

Hoover, Herbert. *The Ordeal of Woodrow Wilson*. New York: McGraw-Hill Book Company, Inc., 1958.

Deeply compassionate commentary by a man who, like Woodrow Wilson, lived through the ordeal of high public office in time of grave national crisis.

House, Edward Mandell. *The Intimate Papers of Colonel House*. Arranged as a Narrative by Charles Seymour, 4 volumes. Boston: Houghton Mifflin Company, 1926–1928.

An invaluable document, though often egotistical, of the close and harmonious friendship between President Wilson and the man "closest to the throne."

Houston, David F. *Eight Years with Wilson's Cabinet*, 2 volumes. Garden City, New York: Doubleday, Page & Company, 1926.

Meticulous and detailed recollections of one of the few men who served in the Cabinet during the entire Wilson administration.

Link, Arthur S. *Wilson, The Road to the White House*. Princeton: Princeton University Press, 1947. *Wilson, The New Freedom*. Princeton: Princeton University Press, 1956. *Wilson, The Struggle for Neutrality*. Princeton: Princeton University Press, 1960.

These three masterly volumes are probably the most scholarly and detailed study so far published on Woodrow Wilson. They cover his life to 1915, and further volumes are in preparation.

McAdoo, Eleanor Wilson. *The Woodrow Wilsons*. New York: The Macmillan Company, 1937.

Intimate and precious details of the private family life of Woodrow and Ellen Wilson and their three daughters, by his youngest daughter.

Tumulty, Joseph P. *Woodrow Wilson as I Know Him.* Garden City, New York: Doubleday, Page & Company, 1921.

A personal memoir of Woodrow Wilson's personal secretary during Wilson's years as Governor of New Jersey and President of the United States.

Walworth, Arthur. *Woodrow Wilson,* 2 volumes. New York: Longmans, Green and Co., 1958.

A highly readable and warm biography emphasizing the personal and human side of Woodrow Wilson.

Wilson, Edith Bolling. *My Memoir.* Indianapolis: The Bobbs-Merrill Company, 1938.

Exceptional recollections of the second Mrs. Wilson, who was First Lady from 1915 to 1920.

Wilson, Woodrow. *The Public Papers of Woodrow Wilson,* 6 volumes, edited by Ray Stannard Baker and William E. Dodd. New York: Harper & Brothers, 1926.

The collected short writings and public speeches of Woodrow Wilson from his college student days to his death.

Supporting Sources

Alexander, James W. *Princeton, Old and New.* New York: Charles Scribner's Sons, 1898.

Bacon, Charles Reade. *A People Awakened.* Garden City, New York: Doubleday, Page & Company, 1912.

Bailey, Thomas A. *Woodrow Wilson and the Lost Peace.* New York: The Macmillan Company, 1944.

Birrell, Francis. *Gladstone.* New York: The Macmillan Company, 1933.

Blum, John M. *Joe Tumulty and the Wilson Era.* Boston: Houghton Mifflin Company, 1951.

Bowers, Claude G. *The Tragic Era, The Revolution After Lincoln.* Boston: Houghton Mifflin Company, 1929.

Burns, James MacGregor. *Roosevelt: The Lion and the Fox*. New York: Harcourt, Brace and Company, 1956.

Collins, Varnum Lansing. *Guide to Princeton, The Town and the University*. Princeton: Princeton University Press, 1920.

Corley, Florence Fleming. *Confederate City, Augusta, Georgia, 1860–1865*. Columbia: University of South Carolina Press, 1960.

Craig, Hardin. *Woodrow Wilson at Princeton*. Norman: University of Oklahoma Press, 1960.

Daniels, Josephus. *Life of Woodrow Wilson*. Philadelphia: The John C. Winston Company, 1924.

Dowdey, Clifford. *The Land They Fought For*. Garden City, New York: Doubleday & Company, Inc., 1955.

Ely, Richard T. *Ground Under Our Feet*. New York: The Macmillan Company, 1938.

French, John C. *A History of the University Founded by Johns Hopkins*. Baltimore: The Johns Hopkins Press, 1946.

Furman, Bess. *White House Profile*. Indianapolis: The Bobbs-Merrill Company, Inc., 1951.

Garraty, John A. *Henry Cabot Lodge*. New York: Alfred A. Knopf, Inc., 1953.

Hagberg, Knut. *Personalities and Powers*. London: John Lane, The Bodley Head, Ltd., 1930.

Hale, William Bayard. *Woodrow Wilson, The Story of His Life*. Garden City, New York: Doubleday, Page & Company, 1912.

Hendrick, Burton J. *The Life and Letters of Walter H. Page*. Garden City, New York: Doubleday, Page & Company, 1925.

Hennig, Helen Kohn. *Columbia, Capital City of South Carolina, 1786–1936*. Columbia: The Columbia Sesqui-Centennial Commission, 1936.

Hoover, Irwin Hood (Ike). *42 Years in the White House*. Boston: Houghton Mifflin Company, 1934.

Hosford, Hester E. *Woodrow Wilson and New Jersey Made Over.* New York: G. P. Putnam's Sons, 1912.

Jones, Charles C., Jr. *Memorial History of Augusta, Georgia.* Syracuse: D. Mason & Co., 1890.

Lander, Ernest McPherson, Jr. *A History of South Carolina, 1865–1960.* Chapel Hill: The University of North Carolina Press, 1960.

Lansing, Robert. *The Big Four and Others of the Peace Conference.* Boston: Houghton Mifflin Company, 1921.

Leckie, George G. (Editor). *Georgia, A Guide to Its Towns and Countryside.* Georgia Board of Education, 1954.

Leech, Margaret. *In the Days of McKinley.* New York: Harper & Brothers, 1959.

Lingle, Walter L. *Memories of Davidson College.* Richmond: John Knox Press, 1947.

Link, Arthur S. *Woodrow Wilson and the Progressive Era, 1910–1917.* New York: Harper & Brothers, 1954.

Lloyd George, Richard (Earl Lloyd George of Dwyfor). *Lloyd George.* London: Frederick Muller, Limited, 1960.

Lorant, Stefan. *The Presidency.* New York: The Macmillan Company, 1951.

McAdoo, William Gibbs. *The Crowded Years.* Boston: Houghton Mifflin Company, 1931.

McElroy, Robert. *Jefferson Davis.* New York: Harper & Brothers, 1937.

Mason, Alpheus Thomas. *Brandeis, A Free Man's Life.* New York: The Viking Press, 1946.

Meigs, Cornelia. *What Makes a College, A History of Bryn Mawr.* New York: The Macmillan Company, 1956.

Moore, Louis T. *Stories Old and New of the Cape Fear Region.* Wilmington, N.C.: privately printed, 1956.

Myers, William Starr (Editor). *Woodrow Wilson, Some Princeton Memories.* Princeton: Princeton University Press, 1946.

Noble, Ransom E., Jr. *New Jersey Progressivism before Wilson.* Princeton: Princeton University Press, 1946.

Nutting, Wallace. *Connecticut Beautiful*. Garden City, New York: Garden City Publishing Company, 1923.

Perkerson, Medora Field. *White Columns in Georgia*. New York: Rinehart & Co., Inc., 1928.

Perry, Bliss. *And Gladly Teach*. Boston: Houghton Mifflin Company, 1935.

Price, Carl F. *Wesleyan's First Century*. Middletown: Wesleyan University, 1932.

Princeton University (by the Trustees). *Memorial Book of the Sesquicentennial Celebration of the Founding of the College of New Jersey*. New York: Charles Scribner's Sons, 1898.

Pringle, Henry F. *The Life and Times of William Howard Taft*. New York: Farrar & Rinehart, Inc., 1939.

Thorp, Willard (Editor). *A Southern Reader*. New York: Alfred A. Knopf, Inc., 1955.

Wertenbaker, Thomas Jefferson. *Princeton, 1746–1896*. Princeton: Princeton University Press, 1946.

White, William Allen. *The Autobiography of William Allen White*. New York: The Macmillan Company, 1946.

Williams, W. E. *The Rise of Gladstone to the Leadership of the Liberal Party*. Cambridge: The University Press, 1934.

Wilson, Woodrow. *An Old Master and Other Political Essays*. New York: Charles Scribner's Sons, 1895. *Congressional Government*. New York: Meridian Books, 1956. *Constitutional Government in the United States*. New York: Columbia University Press, 1908. *Division and Reunion, 1829–1876*. New York: Longmans, Green and Co., 1893. *Leaders of Men*. Princeton: Princeton University Press, 1952. *The New Freedom*. Garden City, New York: Doubleday, Page & Company, 1913. *The State*. Boston: D. C. Heath & Co., 1898.

Works Progress Administration, Federal Writers' Project. *Connecticut, A Guide to Its Roads, Lore, and People*. Boston: Houghton Mifflin Company, 1938. *Georgia, A*

Guide to Its Towns and Countryside. Athens: The University of Georgia Press, 1940. *Virginia, A Guide to the Old Dominion*. New York: Oxford University Press, 1952.

Magazine Articles

The Magazine of Albemarle County History. Viar, Richard E. "Woodrow Wilson at the University of Virginia." 1951–1952.
The Atlantic Monthly. "The Reconstruction of the Southern States." January 1901. Chamberlain, Daniel H. "Reconstruction in South Carolina." April 1901.
Davidson College Bulletin. "Woodrow Wilson and Davidson College." May 1961.
The Georgia Historical Quarterly. Osborn, George C. "Woodrow Wilson as a Young Lawyer, 1882–1883." June 1957.
The Johns Hopkins Alumni Magazine. Latané, John H. "Woodrow Wilson as Student and Lecturer at the Johns Hopkins University." March 1924.
The Ohio Historical Quarterly. Osborn, George C. "Woodrow Wilson's First Romance." January 1958.
Proceedings of the New Jersey Historical Society. Osborn, George C. "Woodrow Wilson and Frederick Jackson Turner." July 1956.
Scribner's Magazine. Wilson, Woodrow. "What Is a College For?" November 1909.
The Wesleyan Argus. "News Notes." January 18, 1889.
The Wesleyan University Alumnus. Price, Carl F. "Woodrow Wilson at Wesleyan." March 1924.

Pamphlets

Lewis, Frank Bell. *Woodrow Wilson's Heritage of Faith*. Staunton: Woodrow Wilson Centennial Commission of Virginia, 1956.
Loth, David. *The Story of Woodrow Wilson*. New York: The Woodrow Wilson Foundation, 1958.

Index

ABOUT THE AUTHOR

Catherine Owens Peare has always been interested in writing. She was the editor of her high school paper, and while studying at New Jersey State College she wrote plays and poetry. After graduation, Miss Peare entered the business world, but she continued to write on evenings and week ends. Her books for young people have been so well received she now devotes all her time to writing.

Miss Peare lives in Norwalk, Connecticut, and travels a great deal throughout Europe, Central America, and the United States, combining pleasure with research for her books.